Low and Moderate Income Housing in the Suburbs

Nina Jaffe Gruen
Claude Gruen
foreword by
William L. C. Wheaton

Prepared by Gruen Gruen + Associates
for and in cooperation with the Miami
Valley Regional Planning Commission

Low and Moderate Income Housing in the Suburbs

An Analysis for the Dayton, Ohio Region

PRAEGER SPECIAL STUDIES IN U.S. ECONOMIC AND SOCIAL DEVELOPMENT

Praeger Publishers   New York   Washington   London

PRAEGER PUBLISHERS
111 Fourth Avenue, New York, N.Y. 10003, U.S.A.
5, Cromwell Place, London S.W.7, England

Published in the United States of America in 1972
by Praeger Publishers, Inc.

Library of Congress Catalog Card Number: 73-176396

Printed in the United States of America

The preparation of this report was financed in
part through an urban planning grant contract
between the Department of Housing and Urban
Development and the Miami Valley Regional
Planning Commission, Dayton, Ohio, under the
provisions of Section 701 of the Housing Act
of 1954, as amended.

MIAMI VALLEY REGIONAL PLANNING COMMISSION

Thomas A. Cloud
Montgomery County, Ohio
Chairman

James A. Ford
Greene County, Ohio
Vice-Chairman

Arthur Haddad
Miami County, Ohio
Treasurer

Members

Gerald Beeman
Bellbrook, Ohio

Jesse Chamberlain
Tipp City, Ohio

Kenneth Cook
Miami County, Ohio

John A. Davis
Centerville, Ohio

Keith Dawson
Gettysburg, Ohio

Virgil P. Deeter
Darke County, Ohio

Ward N. Ditmer
Piqua, Ohio

Leonard Duke
Preble County, Ohio

E. Duncan
Fairborn, Ohio

William Duncan
Yellow Springs, Ohio

John Ernst
Eaton, Ohio

Robert Evans
Phillipsburg, Ohio

Ray Ford
Darke County, Ohio

Raymond Fortune
Trotwood, Ohio

Carl Gerhardt
Moraine, Ohio

Joseph Haines
Greene County, Ohio

Charles Harbottle
Oakwood, Ohio

Dean Harshbarger
Bradford, Ohio

Patrick Hiatt
Versailles, Ohio

Alfred Hintermeister
West Carrollton, Ohio

John Jennens
Brookville, Ohio

Miami Valley Regional Planning Commission Staff
Participating in the Study
Dale F. Bertsch, Executive Director
Stephen C. Nelson, Assistant Director
Ann M. Shafor, Chief, Social Planning and Housing
Kathleen J. Emery, Information Programs Specialist
Minnie F. Johnson, Chief, Research and Information
Roberta Diehl, Associate Planner
Larry L. Perrin, Chief, Mapping and Graphics

Gruen Gruen + Associates Staff
Participating in the Study
Nina J. Gruen, Principal Sociologist: Project Director
Claude Gruen, Principal Economist: Economic and Housing Analyst
Marshall Sylvan, Associate Statistician: Statistical Analyst
Ann Bornstein, Associate Programmer: Information Processing
Ellen Koernig, Research Associate: Data Coordinator
Karen Monkres, Research Assistant: Data Coder
Susan Brown: Interviewer
Debbie Bussinger: Interviewer
Mary Ellen deBrower: Interviewer
Mary Ann Detrick: Interviewer
Beverly Ford: Interviewer
Joyce Herring: Interviewer
Christine Scholl: Interviewer

The Miami Valley Regional Planning Commission Housing Plan--proposed in 1970 and approved unanimously by its Board of locally elected public officials--is surely a milestone in rational, humane, and democratic planning. For the first time in the history of American metropolitan communities, an agreement was reached by a responsible metroplitan body and its constituent local governments on a proposal that would provide low-income families with housing oppor- tunities in the suburbs. These families, now con- centrated largely in the central city of Dayton, were to be offered an opportunity to obtain housing within their means in the suburban areas nearer to new employment locations and with access to more equal community services. The evolution of this plan has been described elsewhere.[*] It reveals a thoughtful and concerned grouped of professional planners, political leaders, and business and communications leaders working together to ascertain the facts, pro- pose reasonable alternative solutions, abate ground- less fears and hostilities, and secure the adoption of equitable policies.

Those policies were designed so that they would not impose extraordinary social costs upon any section of the metropolitan area. Most important to the plan's acceptance was the fact that the number of prospective migrants had been estimated and had been distributed between the counties, cities, and towns of the region, so that each area's share of the total was clearly understood. That understanding provided assurance to the people in each community that they would be assuming only their fair share of the

_____

[*]"A Regional Housing Plan: The Miami Valley Regional Planning Commission Experience," American Institute of Planners' Planners Notebook, Vol. I, No. 1 (April, 1971).

responsibilities involved. Such moral and equitable
guidelines have frequently been persuasive in American
political history, even though persistent and increasing segregation indicates that they are in-
sufficiently persuasive in housing. More important,
however, the allocation also served to convince
each of the communities in the region that its share
involved a manageable number of low-income families
and did not consist of a wholly unmanageable flood
of new migrants. The distributional targets, thus,
by implication, became maximum targets, with the
assurances implied.

In carrying out this remarkable plan, the Commission realized that it needed more information
on the attitudes of both low-income families who
might have opportunities to move to suburban communities and the attitudes of citizens of those communities. The resulting study by Gruen Gruen + Associates is a rare application of social research methods
to the solution of public policy issues. The methods
themselves are scarcely unique. They involve survey
research techniques, which are common in market
analysis, and housing and urban sociological studies.
What is unique is that the several modes of analysis
have been applied to test alternative locational
patterns, public service packages, and social cost
and benefit relationships in a systematic way. In
the housing field, such a combination of analytic and
planning methods is exceedingly rare. One has to
go back to Chester Rapkins's Eastwick housing market
analysis of the mid-1950's to find some equivalent
comprehensiveness, and those studies did not probe
deeply into many of the issues here treated.[*]

The findings illustrate the diversity of preferences that exist in American society and about

_____

[*]Rapkin, Chester and Grigsby, William G.: The
Demand for Housing in Eastwick. A Report prepared
under contract for the Redevelopment Authority of
the City of Philadelphia by the Institute for Urban
Studies, University of Pennsylvania, 1960.

which there is an abundant literature in the field
of housing, sociology, and political science. Low-
income families, black and white, are not anxious
to migrate in large numbers to suburban areas. Many
recognize that the public and private services, and
the friendships that they need, are available primarily in the central city. Some would like to move
to suburbia to get a better environment, better
schools for their children, or other public or private
services. In moving to suburbia, most would prefer
to live in immediate neighborhoods, composed of
people like themselves. Their housing preferences
are quite conventional. They recognize quite real-
istically the extra costs in transportation and
home-maintenance expenditures involved in a move to
suburbia. A few, probably those with middle-class
aspirations, are willing to move into scattered
housing situations, but most would prefer the com-
forts of some more homogeneous relationship.

The preferences of the suburban residents complement these preferences of the poor and black
remarkably well. Suburbanites are concerned to preserve the middle-class image. Most can tolerate
small proportions of low-income families, provided
that the maintenance of the home exterior is assured
and that there is some certainty that the impact on
the school system will not be adverse. They would
prefer to retain presently homogeneous subneighbor-
hoods and associations, the lowest possible property
taxes, the middle-class image, and other elements
of the suburban refuge from the central city. They
have fears generated by stories of mass inundation
and rapid neighborhood change. When confronted with
the prospect of more gradual change, these fears may
be abatable. Political leaders reflect the concerns
of their political constituents.

What is remarkable about this study is the
attempt to probe into the alternatives available
to both the low-income and the suburban groups and
to weigh the tradeoffs that each would make in order
to accommodate the other. Thus, there has been an
attempt, first, to measure preferences and, second,
to analyze the points at which preferences complement

each other and the points at which preferences are in conflict or competition. Finally, there is an interesting effort to devise and measure the trade-offs that different subgroups would prefer it confronted with choices.

Some of these findings are most interesting and new. Others have been sufficiently documented in other studies, so that they verge on common knowledge, even though they are rarely dimensioned. Perhaps most interesting among these findings is the lack of credibility of government institutions. Nobody in the central city or in suburbia really believes in government promises or programs. Overwhelmingly, people distrust the statements of public officials. Under these circumstances, it is hardly surprising that those who have found a refuge from urban problems should resist any change and that those who have found a niche in the slum should be profoundly concerned about moving into a new environment, which, in theory, might be substantially better. Next, as Carl Werthman, Associate Professor of Sociology at The University of California at Berkeley, and others have shown, property maintenance is of overwhelming importance to the suburban image, since it is the symbol of the economic status, the puritan attitudes, the moralities, and the values for which the suburbanite has striven. If this important symbolic element could be controlled, as it might be quite readily, many of the fears of low-income migration to suburbia would be abated.

Another major element in the suburbanities' view, often a controlling one in local policy choices, is the impact of migration on the property tax. There is abundant evidence that, in many jurisdictions, the tax has become so onerous that the electorate is prepared to cut off education for their own children, welfare for their own poor, and health services for their own sick in the interest of avoiding property tax increases. While this problem is one with vastly larger dimensions, it could be resolved selectively in housing policy by subsidies to local taxing authorities to cover the cost of extra services for low-income families. In many communities, even

families in the highest income group are being
excluded by restrictions on the construction of
houses costing less than $30,000, so that the required
selected subsidies might be very substantial.
Alternatively, future forms of revenue sharing might
be conditioned to assure that such funds serve to
cover any real costs occasioned by residential
migration.

Last in this enumeration of major perceived haz-
ards is the matter of school quality. A primary motivation for migration to suburbia on the part of the
middle class is the best possible public education for
their children. Although the public school system
is falling to deliver the expected results in many
ways, even in suburbia, the suburban concern about
this problem is exacerbated by what the public understands to be the near collapse of central city schools
with large populations of low-income and other deprived
students. While the informed public may have heard
of the Coleman Report and its suggestions that
economically and socially integrated schools are the
best guarantors of equality of opportunity in education, particular sectors of the public in suburbia
understandably resist the social costs of such an
approach. Few understand the pedagogical and statisi-
cal arguments involved, and many fear that any break
in the social dike will affect their children profoundly. Perhaps, the best assurance on the score
of quality education is the assurance that the proportion of low-income families will be low, but both
rationality and equity would suggest that a corres-
ponding proportional enrichment program should be
instituted to assure that educational institutions
could respond--if, indeed, the problem solution is
in the domain of education.

One can only hope that this auspicious beginning
is systematically and rigorously monitored to assure
that other metropolitan areas can learn everything
that is possible to learn from the Miami Valley
experience. Clearly, in this field, it is also urgent
that much more detailed data be gathered regarding
the type of houses actually available, the people
actually moving to them, and the compensatory measures

of all sorts actually required to achieve equity. Unfortunately, we have a national tradition that allows an astronaut to be monitored at sixty points on his body continuously for many days of a trip to the moon at a cost of scores of millions of dollars. We have no equivalent policy of monitoring one hopeful public policy experiment at a fraction of that cost, even though it might have far more profound benefits for American society.

If our cities are in trouble today, it is because the nation has committed hundreds of billions of dollars of its research and development resources to atomic energy, atomic destruction, space, war and, domestically, increasing the rate of automobile fatalities. We have systematically failed to engage in the application of our intelligence and our research resources to public policy issues. This book is a splendid illustration of the possibilities for reducing social conflict and achieving indispensable social goals through such research. One can only hope that it will lead to other similar studies with greater depth and follow-through. One can only hope that the Miami Valley Housing Plan succeeds and is imitated elsewhere.

William L. C. Wheaton
Dean, College of Environmental Design
University of California
at Berkeley

ACKNOWLEDGMENTS

In addition to the efforts of the Miami Valley
Regional Planning Commission and Gruen Gruen +
Associates participating staff members, there are
numerous others to whom we owe thanks and without
whose valuable assistance this study could not have
been conducted. First, we would like to thank the
many public officials in the region who took time
out of their busy schedules to share with us their
views and suggestions on the provision of greater
housing opportunity for the region's low- and
moderate-income residents. We would also like to
thank the bankers, real estate brokers, land developers, and builders whose experiences lent insight into
the workings of the regional housing market. We
appreciate the efforts of the national housing experts
who provided us cogent examples of existing housing
projects that are to a greater or lesser degree
successful in mixing differing racial-ethnic groups,
income and sociocultural households, and structure
types. Last, but not least, we would like to thank
the suburbanites and low- moderate-income sample
respondents. It is the attitudes, opinions, and
expectations of the many men and women, young and
old, white and black, married and unmarried, who
consented to be interviewed, which form the sub-
stance of the study. It is these people, after
all, who will determine the future housing opportunities of the region. The government body, the planning
official, or the consultant can merely devise and
institute better catalysts.

While we owe our appreciation to many, the
authors alone are responsible for the contents of
this study.

CONTENTS

Page

SPONSORS OF THE STUDY   v

FOREWORD   ix

ACKNOWLEDGMENTS   xv

LIST OF TABLES AND FIGURES   xxii

LIST OF ABBREVIATIONS   xxv

Chapter

1   THE NEED FOR SUBSIDIZED HOUSING IN
    THE SUBURBS   3

    Relationship Between the Miami Valley
       Regional Housing Plan and This Study   3
    Reasons for Subsidizing Low and
       Moderate Income Housing   6
    Reasons for Building in the Suburbs   10
    Notes   11

2   ATTITUDES AND PREFERENCES OF LOW AND
    MODERATE INCOME HOUSEHOLDS   13

    Reason for Surveying Those Unable To
       Afford New Housing   13
    The Sample   14
    Types of Information Sought   16
    Reactions to Alternative Housing Struc-
       tures   17
    Reactions to Choice Between New Home
       at Present Location or in the Suburbs   25
    Reaction to Economic Integration and
       Shared or Segregated Community Facili-
       ties   29

Chapter   Page

     Reaction to Racial Integration   34
     Notes   36

3   ATTITUDES OF SUBURBAN RESIDENTS TO LOW
     AND MODERATE INCOME HOUSEHOLDS   37

     Reason for Studying the Attitudes of
       the Suburbanites   37
     Information Sought from Suburban Resi-
       dents   39
     The Sample   40
     What the Suburbanites Like About Their
       Suburbs   43
     Observations on Social Factors and
       Social Class   44
     Reactions to Alternative Housing Struc-
       tures   47
     Suburban Responses to Prospect of Low
       and Moderate Income Households in
       Their Community   51
     Inhibitors to Housing Low and Moderate
       Groups in the Suburbs   61
     Notes   65

4   SUBURBAN RESPONSE TO COMPREHENSIVE
     HOUSING PROGRAMS FOR LOW AND MODERATE
     INCOME FAMILIES   67

     Acceptance of Programs by Suburbanites That
       Improve or Safeguard Their Community
       While Providing New Housing for Low
       and Moderate Income Households   67
     Some Governmental Programs Lack Credi-
       bility   69
     Effectiveness of the "Facilitators" in
       Gaining Suburban Acceptance   72
     Suburban Reactions to Alternative Types
       of Low and Moderate Income Housing
       Patterns   75

Chapter   Page

5   ATTITUDES AND PERCEPTIONS OF POLITICIANS
     AND PUBLIC OFFICIALS   79

     The Public Official Survey   79
     Public Officials' Reactions to Struc-
        tural Types   82
     Public Officials' Reactions to Low
        and Moderate Income Groups   85

6   POSSIBLE IMPACTS OF LOW AND MODERATE
     INCOME HOUSING ON THE NEIGHBORHOOD
     ENVIRONMENT   93

     Property Values   94
     Property Maintenance   96
     Property Taxes and General Service
        Levels   100
     School Quality   105
     Social Organization   109
     Social Stability and Status   112
     Notes   116

7   FACTORS THAT MAKE A STABLE MIXED RESI-
     DENTIAL COMMUNITY   119

     A Nationwide Sample of Mixed Residential
        Neighborhoods and Communities   119
     Type of Responses Received   121
     The Nineteen Nominated Areas Grouped by
        Type of Economic Mix   123
     Conclusions Drawn from the National
        Survey   136
     Notes   137

8   WHAT WILL WORK   139

     Directions for Solutions   139
        A Wide Variety of Structural and
           Locational Options   141
        Eventual Home Ownership Generally
           Preferable to Continued Renting   142
        Viable Class Mix Necessary To
           Preserve Neighborhood Stability   143

Informing, Counseling, and Directing
Low and Moderate Income Households
Toward Appropriate Housing Environ-
ments   143
Housing Packages and Support Programs
That Meet Requirements of Low and
Moderate Income Groups and Older
Suburban Residents   144
Credible Programs To Preserve and
Enhance The Suburban Environment   145

9   EXISTING PROGRAMS AND RECOMMENDATIONS
FOR INCREASED SUBURBAN HOUSING   145

Programs and Criteria   147
Wide Variety of Structural and
Locational Possibilities   150
Eventual Home Ownership Possible   151
Viable Class Mix   152
Informing and Counseling Potential
Users   153
Resources and Incentives for Main-
tenance   154
An Even Ratio of Tax Payments to
Public Service Requirements   155
Preserving School Quality   155
Providing for Additionally Needed
Public Services   156
Credibility in Terms of Ability To
Preserve and Enhance the Suburban
Environment   156
Needed Ancillary Programs To Protect
and Improve the Status Quo   158
School Quality   159
Added General Public and Special
Service   160
Need for Another Kind of Housing Pro-
gram   161
Implementation   162
Notes   166

  Page

APPENDIXES   169

APPENDIX A   MVRPC Low/Moderate Income
              Household Survey   171

APPENDIX B   MVRPC Surburbanite Survey   177

APPENDIX C   Summary of the Sampling
              Methodology   191

APPENDIX D   A Description of the Twelve
              Mutually Exclusive Suburban
              Categories   197

APPENDIX E   Suburban Reactions to Low/
              Moderate Income Groups and
              Program Facilitators   199

APPENDIX F   Suburban Reactions to Low In-
              come Groups and Facilitating
              Programs   205

APPENDIX G   Public Official Questionnaire   209

APPENDIX H   National Survey   213

APPENDIX I   Summary Description of the
              Nineteen Areas   217

BIBLIOGRAPHY   227

ABOUT THE AUTHORS   235

LIST OF TABLES AND FIGURES

TABLES

Table   Page

 1   Age of Head of Household   16

 2   Low/Moderate-Income Respondent
       Reactions to Housing Structures   18

 3   Preferences for New House Location   26

 4   Sample Subgroups   28

 5   Breakdown of Responses to Economic
       Integration and Sharing of Facilities
       as per Responses to Locational
       Preferences   31

 6   Choice of Living in Economically In-
       tegrated or Segregated Neighborhoods
       Using Shared or Separate Community
       Institutions   31

 7   Attitudes Toward Racial Integration   35

 8   Suburban Reactions to Housing Structures   49

 9   Least-Liked Structures   50

10   Reasons Given for Feeling that Struc-
       tures Would Harm the Neighborhood or
       Community   52

11   Suburban Reactions to Low/Moderate-
       Income Groups   54

12   Neutral Scores of Suburban Responses to
       Low- and Moderate-Income Groups   57

Table   Page

13   Least-Preferred Lower-Income House-
       holds   58

14   Number of Neutral Average Response
       Scores   60

15   Reasons for Considering Low-/Moderate-
       Income Households   Undesirable Neigh-
       bors   64

16   Respondents Who Question Programs To
       Improve or Preserve Valued Neighbor-
       hood Features   71

17   Average Response Scores when Facili-
       tating Program Elements Are Included,
       Compared to Scores Reflecting Expec-
       tations Concerning the Impact of
       Low- and Moderate-Income Groups
       Making Up 5 Percent of the Neighbor-
       hood's Population when No Such
       Program Elements Are Present   73

18   Suburban Response to Alternative Low-/
       Moderate-Income Housing Patterns   77

19   Public Officials' Projections of Their
       Constituents' Reactions to Structure
       Types   84

20   Public Officials' Projections of Their
       Constituents' Reactions to Low-/
       Moderate-Income Households Comprising
       Less Than 10 Percent of Their Com-
       munities   86

21   Public Officials' Projections of Their
       Constituents' Reactions to Low-/
       Moderate-Income Households Comprising
       at Least 20 Percent of the Community   88

22   Factors That Influence the Rejection of
       Low-/Moderate-Income Groups, Ranked
       by Importance   89

Table   Page

23 Position of Public Officials on
    Alternately Financed Housing
    Programs   91

24 Direct Expenditures by Ohio Local
    Government 1967-68   101

25 Geographical Distribution of Responses   122

26 Characteristics of the Positive Nomi-
    nations as Drawn. from the National
    Survey   125

                    APPENDIX TABLES

1   Suburban Reactions to Low-/Moderate-
    Income Groups and Program Facili-
    tators   201

2   Suburban Reactions to Low-Income
    Groups and Facilitating Programs   207

                        FIGURES

Figure   Page

1   Apartment Dwellings   20

2   Single-Family Residences   22

LIST OF ABBREVIATIONS

DMHA   Dayton Metropolitian Housing
            Authority

FHA   Federal Housing Administration

HAA   Housing Assistance Administration

HUD   Department of Housing and Urban
            Development

MVRPC   Miami Valley Regional Planning
            Commission

VA   Veterans Administration

Low and Moderate
Income Housing
in the Suburbs

1

THE NEED

FOR

SUBSIDIZED HOUSING

IN THE SUBURBS

"There is a geographic dimension to
the regional housing need picture."[1]

RELATIONSHIP BETWEEN THE MIAMI VALLEY
REGIONAL HOUSING PLAN AND THIS STUDY

In July, 1970, the Miami Valley Regional Planning
Commission (MVRPC) issued a housing plan that called
for the federally assisted construction of 14,125
dwelling units for low- and moderate-income households
in the five-county region that includes the city of
Dayton. These units were to be built over a four-year
period throughout all the region's communities, not
just in the run-down neighborhoods of the older cities
and towns that have historically furnished locations
for most federally assisted lower-income housing.
The plan pointed to the fact that Dayton now has virtually the entire region's inventory of public and
assisted housing and suggested that most of the
additionally needed public housing units be built
elsewhere.

The plan had these two principal goals: "To
adequately house all of the region's people. To
create and/or maintain sound, viable neighborhoods
in the process of housing those people."[2]

Analysis of the local housing situation led to the conclusion that these basic goals could not be met unless housing program efforts were bent toward increasing the supply of housing units, especially for low- and moderate-income households, and expanding the range of housing opportunity for everyone geographically.[3] The plan called for placing low- and moderate-income housing units in suburban areas where there might be very little or no such housing present.[4]

The plan was approved by the representatives of the region's communities that sit on the regional planning group as its commissioners. The Dayton Metropolitan Housing Authority (DMHA) agreed to cooperate. The staff of the MVRPC stood ready to work with all community representatives to develop housing in ways that would preserve and enchance the quality of life in the region's communities.

In many suburban communities, however, the response was not universally enthusiastic. Both the MVRPC and the DMHA recognized that, if the plan were to be implemented in a manner that would benefit the entire region, they needed to find out more about the causes of the resistance they perceived. Furthermore, they recognized that successful implementation would require information about the impact of alternative approaches to placing low- and moderate-income housing units in the suburbs.

Therefore, they contracted and cooperated with Gruen Gruen + Associates in the study of the factors that could inhibit the implementation of the plan and the effect of placing low- and moderate-income housing units in suburban areas. The study included a survey of the participants in the local housing processes: A sample of low- and moderate-income families, suburbanites in four areas of the region, local public officials, and businessmen from various branches of the industry that locate, finance, build, and sell housing were interviewed. These interviews were used to ascertain what factors acted as "facilitators" and "inhibitors" in the placing of lower-income housing in suburban neighborhoods and communities and to learn what type of housing and housing patterns the low- and

moderate-income families actually wanted. Housing
experts around the country were also interviewed to
gain information about the effects of the development
of neighborhoods or other areas whose residents differed in their economic, social, or racial characteristics or whose structures differed in the kind of
residences provided (e.g., single-family house, apartment, and so forth). The chapters that follow
summarize the results of these research efforts.

This information has also been analyzed to pre-
dict the kinds of impacts that low- and moderate-
income housing placement can have on the neighborhood
or community features that the suburbanites indicated
they particularly valued. (These effects will vary
with the kind of programs and housing patterns used
to bring the less affluent to the suburbs.) In Chapter
8, the criteria that should be followed if the new
housing is to benefit both the people who will live
in it and the communities in which it is located have
been listed. Finally, these criteria, or directions
for solutions, have been used to evaluate the existing
federal programs, to suggest the need for at least one
new program, and to recommend the kind of implementation that is required.

Much of the information this study presents came
from the people of the Miami Valley region. Thus,
some of the specific research results and planning
recommendations may apply only to this region. However, many of the underlying factors that can impede
or facilitate the expansion of low- and moderate-
income housing opportunities into the suburbs of this
five-county Ohio region apply, also, to the other
metropolitan regions of the United States.

It is believed by us that much of what motivated
the MVRPC to call for the expansion of such opportunities has a parallel in other regions. The MVRPC
did not call for the development of subsidized housing
in the suburbs because it wanted to engage in social
engineering: It called for such action in order to
improve the quality and quantity of housing available
to the expanding population of this growing region
and to encourage land-use patterns that would benefit
this and future generations.

The purpose of the research and analysis done by
us can best be understood if some of the factors that
led the Miami Valley planners to make the expansion
of low- and moderate-income housing opportunities a
critical element in their housing program are first
summarized, that is, if two questions are first
answered: Why subsidize new housing for those too
poor to buy it on their own? Why locate any of these
dwellings in the suburbs?

REASONS FOR SUBSIDIZING LOW
AND MODERATE INCOME HOUSING

In a December, 1970, article in The American
Economic Review, Henry Aaron of the Brookings Insti-
tution reported on his research concerning income
taxes and housing:

> The Internal Revenue Code contains massive
> tax subsidies for housing. The largest
> accrue to homeowners through exemption from
> taxation of net imputed rent and deducti-
> bility of mortgage interest and property
> taxes paid. Smaller benefits accrue to
> owners of rental housing to the extent that
> accelerated depreciation exceeds true
> depreciation on real estate by a greater
> margin than accelerated depreciation on
> other properties.[5]

Aaron notes that, while these tax benefits offer
substantial subsidies to the middle- and upper-income
households who can buy houses or rental units, they
do not help those who own neither. He and other
researchers into this subject also point out that the
gains from these subsidies rise with one's tax bracket
and have no effect if income is so low that the tax-
payer takes a standard deduction.[6] The U.S. Treasury
Department estimates that the deduction of interest
on mortgages of owner-occupied homes results in a
revenue loss to it of $2.8 billion per year; the
deductibility of property taxes by this same group
is estimated to result in an annual loss of $2.9
billion.[7] It is not suggested that these subsidies

are not desirable but merely that they do exist.

In addition to these sizable tax subsidies,
upper- and middle-class home and apartment owners
also benefit from the federal government's heavy
involvement in the mortgage market, both as an insurer
and a manipulator. The provision of grants to bring
roads, utilities, and sewer service into areas where
new housing is being built also works to reduce the
cost of these houses to the middle- and upper-income
families that can afford to pay for their construction.
Through the period ending December 31, 1968, the
Department of Housing and Urban Renewal, (HUD) had paid
out $1.27 million in sewer and water grants alone.[8]

If any low- and moderate-income households are
to be able to occupy new homes, they will need a
different type of subsidy than those discussed above.
They will need direct subsidies, because they have
neither the income nor the credit to pay the costs
of building new homes. Until recently, the only
form in which such subsidies were given was the public
housing program. In April, 1969, there were 744,496
dwelling units under public housing management. This
older program, plus those that have been added more recently and are discussed in Chapter 9, cost the
federal government less than $500 million in 1970.[9]

Thus, even if direct subsidies for low- and
moderate-income housing were to be doubled over their
present levels, they would still not equal the indirect
federal housing subsidies granted to the more affluent
members of our society. Should direct subsidies to
those with lower incomes be continued or even increased, they would still be neither the exclusive
nor the largest receivers of governmental housing
subsidies. This observation is made to put the
question of direct subsidies into perspective, not
to suggest that because housing incentives for one
group are paid for indirectly, direct incentives
should provided for other groups.

The argument for subsidy rests simply on the pro-
position that the society in which we live should de-
vote some of its efforts to <u>directly</u> meeting the housing

needs of the families now living in low-quality
dwellings. These families cannot generate the "effective demand" for new housing--that is, they cannot
afford to pay what it costs to build even the least
expensive standard unit. Thus, as the Miami Valley
regional planners realized, and as Frank S. Kristoff
observed in his work for the National Commission on
Urban Problems:

> The concept of housing need is a social,
> not a market, criterion. It is embodied
> in the definition of the national housing
> objective in the Housing Act of 1949. In
> part, it includes the elimination of sub-
> standard and other inadequate housing . . .
> and . . . a decent home and suitable living
> environment for every American family.[10]

Thus, those who argue for direct subsidies must say--
all of our citizens should live in decent housing
because we as a nation can afford to let them do so,
whether they as individuals can or cannot afford to
do so.

Historically, even if lip service has been given
to, or if Americans have believed in, the concept of
housing need, the nation has still continued to let
the low- and moderate-income families obtain their
housing from the nation's stock of used housing.
Many have argued that it was much more efficient to
let those with effective demand pay for the new
housing and then to let their old houses "filter
down" to those who had the need but not the demand.
But housing quality can also "filter down" with the
price of the housing, unless conditions in the local
housing market work to preclude this.

The market conditions that are required to keep
the quality of our least expensive older housing
stock from dropping are similar to those needed to
maintain the quality of used cars or any other product
with a reasonably long life potential that is resold
or rented on an open market. If the demand grows
more quickly than the supply of the used product
available for rent or sale, prices start to climb

and quality drops. Conversely, if the sellers or
lessors find that they have more of the product
available than is demanded at current price and
quality levels, they are forced to lower their prices
and keep quality up.11

     There is evidence that existing conditions in
the regional housing market will not push the quality
of the older used housing up. Vacancies are low, and
the pressure of highway construction, urban renewal,
and the land needs of commercial uses chips away at
the supply of housing in the neighborhoods where these
older units exist. The amount of overcrowding and
present use of dilapidated structures by households
with incomes below $4,000 provides strong evidence
of heavy demand for the older and least expensive
units available.12

     Thus, the condition of the region's stock of
older, cheaper housing will tend to suffer further
declines in quality in future years because of the
shortage of such older units. The gap between the
price of these units and the cost of newly built,
nondirectly subsidized housing is very great. Therefore, if this shortage is attacked merely by building
more units in the newer neighborhoods, the resulting
"trickle down" in supply will not compete with the
older, cheaper stock for many years to come.

     Even if enough new nondirectly subsidized housing
could be built to quickly affect the stock of older
housing at the bottom of the present price range,
the manner in which this would have to happen might
not be universally acceptable. Housing does not
"filter down" in price or quality on a random house-
by-house basis; instead, the housing product shifts
price and quality on a neighborhood-by-neighborhood
basis. Thus, any attempt to provide improved housing
for the poor by a massive injection of housing for
the more well-to-do would have to work by dramatically
accelerating the process of neighborhood change.
This is not what the MVRPC plan seeks to do. It wants
to support neighborhoods that presently provide
desirable housing environments--not hurry their
transfer to a new set of occupants.

The plan encourages the rehabilitation of units
in existing neighborhoods, but recognizes that such
encouragement can be most effective if market pressures for higher quality operate concurrently with
government incentives. Its call for directly subsidized units is an attempt to create such pressures,
while it simultaneously supplies the need of those
currently unable to afford decent housing.

REASONS FOR BUILDING IN THE SUBURBS

Efforts to ameliorate undesirable conditions
and to prevent further degeneration of our housing
stock cannot succeed if they continue to be limited
to the older neighborhoods of our cities and towns.
First, these neighborhoods have relatively little
open land, and, thus, the construction of new housing
frequently requires the demolition of the older.
Such demolition and rebuilding is not only expensive,
but also works to inhibit the raising of vacancy
rates in the older neighborhoods, where the lower-
income families now live. This, in turn, holds back
the market forces needed to encourage the private
maintenance and rehabilitation of older buildings.
In other words, it precludes the double-barreled
effect attainable by leaving the older units to
compete with new ones.

In addition to avoiding these constraints of
land and building, the use of suburban lands permits
a scaling down of neighborhood size and the removal
of socially and psychologically healthy families from
undesirable influences. Most of the central city
sites that have attracted subsidized building in
the past have been near or within blighted areas.
The new buildings can seldom alter the environmental
effect created by the larger area. Nor is it easy
to build housing in such areas without crowding
inhabitants who are able to adjust to the economic
and social requirements of our society close to those
who cannot.

Still another reason to build such housing in
the suburbs is because, to an ever increasing extent,

that is where the jobs are. Industrial and other
employment opportunities have been moving to the
suburbs with increasing speed since the mid-1950's.
This is certainly true in the greater Dayton area.
If the lower-income households that used to find
jobs in the central city are not allowed to move as
their job opportunities do, the result can only be
to encourage what Herman P. Miller defines as poverty:
"Poverty in its truest sense is more than mere want;
it is want mixed with a lack of hope."[13]

Finally, it is becoming increasingly clear that
a failure to provide housing opportunities for the
lower-income, primarily black households, currently
confined to the urban centers, will eventually result
in a nation of low-income center cities and separate
suburban communities, inhabited by higher-income,
primarily white households. Thus, the urban centers
will no longer serve their historic function as a
catalyst to social interaction. America will be the
poorer for this loss. Along with this very important
societal loss will be the misuse of valuable land
resources. Many surburban communities, in their
attempts to keep out the less affluent, will continue
to institute large-lot zoning, thus using up land
that should kept for future generations. Although
this study was initiated in the spirit of John F.
Kennedy's words: "Just because there's a problem
doesn't mean there's a solution," it was accepted
that it was necessary to find beneficial ways to
provide greater suburban housing opportunities to
the low- and moderate-income households.

NOTES

1. Miami Valley Regional Planning Commission,
A Housing Plan for the Miami Valley Region (July,
1970), p. 18.

2. Ibid., p. 3.

3. Ibid., p. 4.

4. Ibid., p. 12.

5. Henry Aaron, "Income Taxes and Housing,"
The American Economic Review (December, 1970), p.
802.

6. See, for example, Richard E. Slitor, "The
Federal Income Tax in Relation to Housing," Research
Report No. 5 (Washington, D.C.: National Commission
on Urban Problems, 1968).

7. Letter from Gerard M. Brannon, Associate
Director of the Treasury Department Office of Tax
Analysis, September 2, 1970.

8. Committee on Banking and Currency, Subcom-
mittee on Housing and Urban Affairs, "Progress Report
on Federal Housing and Urban Development Programs"
(Washington, D.C.: U.S. Government Printing Office,
March, 1970), p. 91.

9. U.S. Department of Commerce, Bureau of the
Census, Statistical Abstract of the United States
(91st ed.; Washington, D.C.: U.S. Government Printing
Office, 1970), p. 381.

10. Frank S. Kristoff, "Urban Housing Needs
Through the 1980s, an Analysis and Projection,"
Research Report No. 10 (Washington, D.C.: National
Commission on Urban Problems, 1968), p. 8.

11. For a more detailed discussion of the
quality determinants, see Claude Gruen, "The Socio-
Economic Determinants of Urban Residential Housing
Quality, (unpublished Ph.D dissertation, Department
of Economics, University of Cincinnati, 1964).

12. Miami Valley Regional Planning Commission,
Housing Needs in the Miami Valley Region 1970-1975
(June, 1970).

13. Herman P. Miller, Rich Man, Poor Man, (New
York: Thomas Y. Crowell Company, 1971), p. 111.

2

**ATTITUDES
AND PREFERENCES
OF LOW
AND MODERATE INCOME
HOUSEHOLDS**

"Glad Someone Started Asking
Instead of Telling"[1]

REASON FOR SURVEYING THOSE UNABLE
TO AFFORD NEW HOUSING

To many persons, hopefully, the reason for
surveying those unable to afford new housing is
obvious. The poor are the people who will live in
the new suburban housing whose construction is to be
encouraged by governmentally supported programs and
policies. It is absurd to plan housing for any group
without considering the needs and preferences of the
group. No private builder or developer operating in
a competitive market could so neglect his consumers:
His failure to perceive the preferences of potential
buyers would cause them to take their housing dollars
elsewhere. However, there is usually no such constraint upon subsidized housing produced for low-
and moderate-income households. At least historically, the production of directly subsidized housing
has been far too small to satisfy the demands of
those who were eligible for it. Therefore, there
was no competition, and those too poor to buy
nondirectly subsidized housing were forced to take
whatever was produced for them, wherever it was
located.

So, directly subsidized housing for the poor
and for moderate-income households has been used
whether or not the housing fits the physical needs,
tastes, and life-style preferences of the users.
Frequently, such programs have benefited neither the
occupants nor society as a whole. Since the government first began to build directly subsidized public
housing projects, the cry has frequently been heard:
"Things didn't work out the way we planned." These
past "errors" are then studied by the developers of
new programs to avoid their repetition. But such
studies do not provide sufficient information for
the formulation of effective new programs. They
cannot properly evaluate the full range of possibilities in the light of user requirements. To get such
information, one must study the housing preferences
and attitudes of those who will be served by the
programs. That is what the MVRPC and the DMHA asked
us to do. They wanted to know how the people they
are planning for want to live, as they evaluate and
conceptualize programs to serve these people.

THE SAMPLE

Face-to-face interviews were held, with 214
respondents, drawn from a sample of low- and moderate-
income households in Dayton, Ohio. There was no
attempt to include a proportionate number of all the
different kinds of low- and moderate-income households
in the region in the sample. People were not being
polled as to how they would vote on different housing
issues. Instead, the staff of the MVRPC and Gruen
Gruen + Associates worked to develop a sample
representing the major groups now living in the central city who would be expected to use the low- and
moderate-income housing that the plan contemplates.

The low-income individuals to be sampled were
to be selected from households that earned less than
$5,000 per year--half from black households and half
from white. The moderate-income individuals were to
be drawn from households whose income ranged from
$5,000-$10,000 per year--again with a fifty-to-fifty
racial mix.

The sample for households earning less than
$5,000 a year was to be drawn at random from the
DMHA's waiting list. However, the list turned out
to be an imperfect source of a low-income sample for
two reasons: First, while the list worked well for
locating poor families in black neighborhoods, many
of the addresses given in white neighborhoods were
for vacant houses or demolished buildings. Therefore,
to augment the sample, the MVRPC randomly selected
addresses in low-income white neighborhoods. Secondly,
some of the respondents whose names were taken from
the DMHA list reported in the interview that their
annual household incomes exceeded $10,000. This does
not mean that they lied to get on the list, since
it is entirely possible that either husband or wife,
or both, were unemployed when they were listed but
that subsequently, either one or both found jobs.

The sample of households in the $5,000-$10,000
yearly income category was drawn by using the Deed
Records Manuals to locate Dayton streets where
people within this category could be expected to
live. All house numbers on the selected streets were
then listed from the city directory, and a random
sample was taken from the list.

The obtained sample of central city residents
contained 54 percent white and 46 percent black
households. Of the individuals we actually interviewed, 40 percent reported their household incomes
to be less than $5,200 per year; 34 percent had
incomes between $5,200 and $10,400; and 19 percent
had incomes exceeding $10,400. The black and white
households included in the sample did not differ
significantly from each other in regard to income.
However, the two racial groups did differ in terms
of age, as indicated by Table 1.

Of all the households in the sample, 67 percent
contained more than one wage earner. Sixty-one percent
of those workers had jobs within five miles of their
present residence, and 27 percent of the workers
traveled between five and twenty-five miles to their
jobs. It was not possible to get exact information
about the distance to work of 11 percent of the

TABLE 1

Age of Head of Household
(In Percent)

Age	White	Black
Under 30	26	26
31-45	29	37
46-60	22	25
Over 61	27	12

breadwinners whose households were surveyed. The
majority of employed drove to work (75 percent,
including 7 percent who ride with someone else); 16
percent indicated they generally rode the bus, while
only 5 percent walked to work.

While most people use a car for work travel,
the bus is used more frequently (44 percent) than
the automobile (29 percent) by those households
seeking social services outside the home. Another
22 percent walk to obtain such services. The Welfare
Department, the medical clinic, and the Dayton Boys
Club are routine destinations of 7 percent of the
sample. Many more of these households are welfare
recipients, but most of these transactions are handled
by mail.

TYPES OF INFORMATION SOUGHT

A copy of the interview questionnaire is included
in Appendix A. Each respondent was encouraged to
make comments, in addition to answering the questions.
Immediately before, and again after, the administration
of the questionnaire, the respondents were told that
the interview was in no way a promise of new housing.
The carefully trained and periodically debriefed

interviewers explained that the information they
received would be used in planning for people like
the respondents; thus, it was important for the
respondents to fully and accurately reveal their own
attitudes and preferences.

The interviewers asked respondents to make
choices regarding the following types of options:

1.   A series of eight pictures showing different
single- and multifamily buildings that could be produced within the cost limitations of existing programs
designed to provide low- and moderate-income housing

2.   A central city location or a suburban location

3.   Economically heterogeneous or homogeneous
neighbors, with shared or unshared community facilities

4.   Interracial living or nonintegrated neighborhoods.

REACTIONS TO ALTERNATIVE
HOUSING STRUCTURES

As indicated above, each respondent was shown
a series of eight photographs. The first four
illustrated a variety of multifamily structures,
including a high rise and a townhouse. The last
four showed single-family homes, varying in design
from modern to traditional. Each is an existing
structure in the Miami Valley Region, serving either
low- or moderate-income households. The responses
to the eight pictures are presented in Table 2. The
four apartment units are shown in Figure 1 and the
four single-family homes in Figure 2.

Almost all the interviewees indicated that, if
given the choice, they would prefer a single-family
dwelling to an apartment. This strong yearning to
live in their own home was associated with the desire
for more personal freedom than they felt was possible
in the average apartment unit.

TABLE 2

Low-/Moderate-Income Respondent Reactions
To Housing Structures
(In Percent)
(a)
Single Family

Picture Number	Most Liked	Second Most Liked	Least Liked
5	13	20	15
6	39	38	1
7	4	3	75
8	42	35	5
No Choice	2	3	3
Total	99*	99*	99*

(b)
Multifamily

Picture Number	Most Liked	Second Most Liked	Least Liked
1	41	25	6
2	17	38	11
3	3	8	76
4	36	24	4
No Choice	3	5	3
Total	100	100	100

*Totals do not equal 100 percent due to rounding.

Single-family dwellings shown as Structures 8
and 6 are the preferred houses. Structure 8 is a
one-story brick house with a modified ranch-style
appearance, complete with white trim, shutters, and
mullioned windows, which give it a strongly traditional flavor. It is probably most representative
of the style preference of Dayton's suburban residents.

Structure 6 is a frame and brick veneer home,
one story in height, and is typical of much of the
Dayton area's suburban development. Common characteristics are the L-shaped plan, the large aluminum
windows, and the wrought-iron porch trim.

Reactions to Structure 7, the only modern alternative, were almost uniformly negative. Part of this
negativism may be attributed to the picture itself,
which, unfortunately, does not show the entire house.*
Structure 7 is a two-story, single-family home,
marked by bold massing, sweeping roof lines, and
dark-colored vertical wood siding. The lack of
windows was perceived as particularly threatening--
in fact, a female interviewee said that the house
"looked dangerous," since people could "attack you
at the front door," with the occupants unable to see
them. Another commented that the house "just didn't
make sense without windows." There were numerous
statements concerning the dwelling's barnlike"
appearance. Still others found it "boxlike," closed
in," and "dark-looking." Few low-moderate-income
households approved of its modernness.

Multifamily Structure 2 and single-family
Structure 5 did not elicit as many responses, either
positive or negative. These structures registered
as more ordinary and were, for the most part, ignored.
Structure 5 is a one-story home of wood and brick
construction and of contemporary design. The color

----

*In future studies, care should be taken to
have all pictures shot from the same angle and with
equivalent landscapes.

FIGURE 1
Apartment Dwellings

Structure 1

Structure 2

Structure 3

Structure 4

FIGURE 2
Single-Family Residences

Structure 5

Structure 6

Structure 7

Structure 8

and materials used in it make it an acceptable, if
unexciting, version of a ranch-style home. Structure
2 is a townhouse building of brick and frame construction, and it is more modern in design than
Structure 1. The use of a mansard roof, punctuated
by the clean vertical lines of the windows, is charac-
teristic of this recently popular townhouse style.
Functionally, it is probably similar to Structure 1,
but its visual effect is quite different.

Structures 1 and 4 were selected most frequently
as the preferred multifamily buildings. Structure
1 is of townhouse or row house design; each unit is
two stories high, with a separate entrance. To maxi-
mize the feeling of individual dwellings, the facade
treatments vary in color, type of materials, porch
overhangs, and fenestration. This structure is most
frequently preferred by respondents in the low- and
moderate-income sample. They saw it as "clean,"
"uncluttered," "homey," "more separated," "a place
for common people," and "fitting in their neighborhood."

Structure 4 was the second most frequent selection
from among the multifamily options. It is a garden
apartment building, with the appearance of a townhouse. It is an older building that has been skill-
fully and attractively remodeled and still blends
with its neighborhood. The modified mansard roof,
arches, and brick combine to make it appealing and
comfortable looking. The people who were interviewed
said they liked the "brick" facade and that this
structure gave them a "warm feeling"; some liked it
because it "looked exclusive."

Structure 3 is the only example of a high-rise
building used in the survey. It is eleven stories
high, of buff brick, and has strong vertical accents,
which are especially apparent when it is lighted at
night. The design is enhanced by the use of arches
at the top and bottom of the building; these have
almost become its trademark.* Because this is the

----

*The arches are partially obscured in the picture.

only high-rise building in this part of Dayton, it
contrasts conspicuously with its surroundings, in
spite of its overall attractiveness and its setting
overlooking a small, tree-fringed lake. Few other
apartment buildings in the Dayton area boast the
same amenities; it has won awards for its quality as
a senior citizens' housing development. Nevertheless,
the sample was almost uniformly opposed to this
structure. All of their comments centered on the
density implied by such a building. One respondent
said that she "doesn't like high places because
there's no air there." Quite a few indicated they
"did not want so many people over them." Several
complained that "it's hard to get acquainted in such
a structure." Many of the negative feelings were
expressed in comparisons with hotels and office
buildings.

REACTIONS TO CHOICE BETWEEN NEW HOME AT PRESENT LOCATION OR IN THE SUBURBS

Each interviewee in the sample of low- and
moderate-income households was asked the following
question:

"If you had the following two choices, which
would you pick: a) A new home in this immediate area
or b) A new home outside the city somewhere in the
suburbs?"

Of the total sample, 51 percent preferred a
new home in their own neighborhood--and 44 percent
preferred a new home in the suburbs; 5 percent were
indifferent as to location, as long as they received
a new home. White respondents were far more receptive
to living in the suburbs than were black households,
who tended to prefer their present central city
neighborhoods (see Table 3).

For those households preferring to remain where
they are, the black households appeared to be most
concerned with maintaining their present neighbors,
while more white households indicated satisfaction
and fondness for their present home.

TABLE 3

Preferences for New House Location
(In Percent)

Location Preferred	White Households	Black Households
Prefer Own Neighborhood	43	61
Prefer Suburb	53	34
Indifferent to Location	4	5
Total	100	100

Generally speaking, the white households in the sample showed a stronger desire to live away from the central city than did the black, who seem to be more adapted to an urban way of life. This generalization can be drawn from the following typical comments. A black female respondent said: "The reason I don't prefer the suburbs is because things are closer here--the schools and the things children go to. Transportation is easier." Another said: "Suburban location too far out for working parents-- would knock them out of good privileges--counties doesn't provide parks with supervisors--they would feel inferior and they couldn't keep yards like ones there." A third "didn't know what it's like to live in the suburbs. Always lived here--never wanted to move, enjoy neighborhood."

That a large percentage of black households prefer their present location cannot be interpreted solely as a fear of the unfamiliar, though this certainly plays a part for all groups. For the black community, their neighbors not only provide them primary means of socializing but, also, a sense of security through mutual aid. A neighbor can be counted on to lend a cup of sugar, a dollar till payday, or babysitting services in the expectations such favors will be returned. For many poor blacks, this is their primary source of capital.

Just as there is more than one reason why persons prefer to remain where they are, there is also a variety of reasons--both realistic and unrealistic-- why particular households chose a suburban location. Some seek the nirvana of complete privacy, not realizing the proximity to neighbors common in most suburban areas. One young man said: "I feel like houses in general are too close together. Neighbors often object to dogs and my car business." This respondent's front yard contains several old automobiles and automobile parts, which he uses to make repairs, furnishing him with an important source of added revenue. He also commented: "Most people around here are in different age brackets, which also makes it difficult."

Several respondents preferring a suburban location equated the suburban option with "ruralness." These households indicated their desire to "raise chickens" and do a little farming, particularly for home-consumed products. Some of these households were from Appalachia and missed the farmland and privacy they had previously enjoyed.

Other attributes associated with the suburbs in the minds of some of the low- and moderate-income households are the trees, the cleaner air, cooler climate, larger yards, and overall beauty. Still others conceive it as an area of quiet and increased safety. A few perceive the suburbs as providing an avenue of upward mobility for themselves and their children. However, many are frightened that the niceties will cost them too much in terms of maintenance and afraid, also, of the problems of "keeping up with the Joneses."

These general findings suggest why these individuals feel as they do, but they most definitely should not be read to suggest that these households are uniform in their preferences and attitudes. However, somewhat greater uniformity of attitudes was found when the responses were grouped and analyzed according to the various subgroups in the total sample. This suggests that the low- and moderate-income residents who share demographic characteristics also tend to have similar attitudes.

The low- and moderate-income sample was statis-
tically grouped into eight categories. The categories
and the number and percentage of sample respondents
falling into each are listed in Table 4.

All subsequent tables that summarize the attitudes
of the low- and moderate-income households are based
on the assumption that each subgroup makes up 100
percent of the sample. In other words, the statistical program separately calculates the responses of
each of the subgroups.

An analysis of the responses of eight subgroups
from within the low- and moderate-income sample, excluding the four elderly and physically handicapped
groups, shows that the majority of the following
three groups prefer new dwelling units in the immediate
neighborhood to new units in the suburbs: low-income
black with husband, moderate-income black with husband,
and low-income white with husband.

TABLE 4

Sample Subgroups

Low-/Moderate-Income Households	Number	Percent
Low-Income White--No Husband	15	7
Low-Income White--Husband	38	18
Low-Income Black--No Husband	15	7
Low-Income Black--Husband	19	9
Moderate-Income White--No Husband	3	1
Moderate-Income White--Husband	60	28
Moderate-Income Black--No Husband	6	3
Moderate-Income Black--Husband	58	27
Total	214	100

The moderate-income black group with no husbands was equally divided on the choice of new housing in their present location versus living in the suburbs. A majority of the other households with no husband said they would prefer a new house in the suburbs. However, while almost all of the white low-income respondents with no husband, and a substantial proportion of the moderate-income white husbandless respondents preferred the suburbs, only a slight majority of the low-income blacks with no husbands shared this preference. The preference for the suburbs shown by three out of the four husbandless groups may reflect their desire to live in an environment that is less hostile to such households and their belief that the suburbs they have not seen would offer them such respite.

Of households with husbands, the only subgroup with a majority preferring the suburbs is that with moderate income--and the majority is slight.

REACTION TO ECONOMIC INTEGRATION AND SHARED OR SEGREGATED COMMUNITY FACILITIES

The interviewers posed the following options to each respondent in the sample of low- and moderate-income central Dayton residents--to be answered regardless of the interviewee's opinion as to the merits of such locations for new housing:

a) Living in new low and moderate housing units which are not clustered together, but scattered among the existing suburban residential neighborhoods? In this situation most of your neighbors would have higher incomes.

b) Living in a separate neighborhood made up of new housing units for low- and moderate-income families. The immediate neighborhood would be composed of families with roughly the same incomes. However, the neighborhood residents would use the same community facilities, including

schools, used by all other neighborhoods
in the city or township.

c) Living in a separate neighborhood made
up of new housing units for low and
moderate income families. The immediate
neighborhood would be composed of families
with roughly the same incomes, with the
neighborhood residents having their own
community facilities, including schools.

The response to the options posed in this question demonstrate that, if housing opportunity is to
be provided to the region's low- and moderate-income
households, then these households must be given
alternate locational and neighborhood choices. The
preferences of the total sample were analyzed, and
the responses of various low- moderate-income sub-
categories were noted.

Of all low- and moderate-income respondents, 56
percent indicated a preference for living in a separate neighborhood with families of roughly the same
income groups but sharing in the institutions and
community facilities of adjoining higher income
neighborhoods. Sixty-four percent of all black
households and 48 percent of all white households in
the sample gave this response.

Responses to these options were also tabulated
on the basis of responses given to the previously
discussed choice of locations for a new home in suburbia or near their present location. Table 5 presents
the results. They do not differ dramatically from
the results of the total sample. However, more of
those households favoring a new home in the immediate
area preferred a separate neighborhood with shared
institutions than did those who chose a suburban
home, while one-fifth of the latter chose a completely
socially separated suburban living environment.

Most of the respondents in each low- and
moderate-income household subgroup that we analyzed
separately did prefer the separate neighborhood with
shared institutions. However, as shown in Table 6,

TABLE 5

Breakdown of Responses to Economic Integration and Sharing
of Facilities as per Responses to Locational Preferences
(In Percent)

Preferred New Home Location	Option A-- Scatteration	Option B-- Separate Neighborhood. Shared Institutions	Option C-- Separate Neighborhood, with Own Institutions	No Preferance	Total
Immediate Area	24	60	7	9	100
Suburbs	27	51	20	2	100

TABLE 6

Choice of Living in Economically Integrated or Segregated
Neighborhoods Using Shared or Separate Community Institutions
(In Percent)

Subgroup of Low- and Moderate- Income Interviewees	Prefer Option A-- Scatteration	Prefer Option B-- Separate Neighborhood Shared Institutions	Prefer Option C-- Separate Neighborhood, Own Institutions	Total
Low-Income White--No Husband	29	50	21	100
Low-Income White--Husband	24	61	15	100
Low-Income Black--No Husband	21	64	15	100
Low-Income Black--Husband	21	74	5	100
Moderate-Income White--No Husband	33	67	0	100
Moderate-Income White--Husband	36	48	16	100
Moderate-Income Black--No Husband	0	67	33	100
Moderate-Income Black--Husband	26	63	11	100
Total Sample	26	56	13	95*

*Of the total sample, 5 percent were indifferent as to location.

there were significant differences in the cluster
of preferences between the various types of low- and
moderate-income households.

Sixty-three percent of those who responded and
were black, with moderate incomes, and living in
households with husbands preferred economically
homogeneous neighborhoods with shared institutions.
This was also the preference of 67 percent of both
the moderate-income blacks and whites with no husbands
and 74 percent of low-income blacks with husbands;
with only one subgroup--moderate-income whites with
husband--was there less than a majority of respondents preferring this option. On an income basis,
it appears that respondents from households earning
between $3,400 and $7,800 per year were most likely
to select this option.

In contrast, the option of living with higher-
income households was most likely to appeal to those
sampled households with incomes exceeding $7,800
per year. When those who would not answer or were
indifferent to this option as a separate group were
considered, it was found that 26 percent of the
respondents preferred to live in scattered low- and
moderate-income housing units located in higher-income
neighborhoods. Slightly more whites (28 percent)
than blacks (22 percent) selected this option. The
fact that those who preferred this option were most
likely to be drawn from the upper end of the moderate-
income spectrum suggested that those who most wanted
to live with higher-income households also were the
most likely to be upwardly mobile.

An elderly white woman who selected this option
said it was "a great idea for people who want to get
out--better when older--area here driving me crazy,
cars noise and children." A middle-aged black pro-
ponent said "I'm for it, there are a lot of black
people who need them, and it's hard for them to
find nice houses for a low price." Many of those
respondents rejecting option A agreed with the
woman who was concerned that she "couldn't compete
with them--couldn't afford to keep up property."

The smallest percent (13 percent) preferred to live in neighborhoods with persons of roughly equivalent incomes and to maintain their own institutions and facilities including schools; 14 percent of the white and 11 percent of the black households selected this option. This alternative tended to appeal to the lowest-income (less than $3,400 per year) and highest-income (more than $8,000 per year) households. Many of the households preferring this third option made it clear that they were interested in class, not racial homogeneity. One respondent stated that it "was better for people because classes don't necessarily like living together. Not races but people of different standards." Another woman put it this way:

> I think it would be a good idea to find
> a new section to build a new community.
> Prefer to see it integrated racially,
> which would keep balance in schools; since
> we're here together we might as well learn
> to live together. Do not prefer income
> integration because people tend to try to
> keep up with Joneses when they can't
> afford it.

Approximately 69 percent of the low- and moderate-income Dayton residents interviewed selected one of the two options of living in a separate neighborhood made up of new housing units for low- and moderate-income families. About 5 percent did not select one of the options and about 26 percent wanted to live with higher-income households. The findings suggest that the majority of Dayton's low- and moderate-income residents would expect economically dissimilar neighbors to have the problems that Herbert Gans discovered when he studied Levittown: "Income similarity is valued by the less affluent, not as an end in itself, but because people who must watch every penny cannot long be comfortable with more affluent neighbors, particularly when children come home demanding a toy or clothes they have seen next door."[2]

However, while the majority valued neighborhood
income similarity and a minority sought higher-income
neighbors, all desired high-quality housing and
community facilities.

REACTION TO RACIAL INTEGRATION

Fifty-seven percent of the total sample stated
a preference to live in a racially integrated environment. Forty percent preferred to live among members
of their own race exclusively. The remaining 3
percent were indifferent on the question. However,
black households were far more willing to live with
those of other races (81 percent) than were white
households (40 percent).

The disparity in attitudes toward racial integration that is exhibited by white and black, low-
and moderate-income Dayton residents is not unexpected.
It is probably true that white attitudes are changing
in the direction of accepting racial integration,
while some young blacks are becoming more inclined
toward racial separatism. But the attitudes that
were found still reflect the general prevalence of
racism, which is explained by Joshua A. Fishman, as
follows:

> On the whole, however, Negroes remain much
> more positive toward themselves, their
> neighbors and the entire community regard-
> less of all the vicissitudes of inter-
> racial living. After all is said and done
> an interracial suburban neighborhood is a
> step up for most Negroes. Any white who
> is appreciably concerned for his status in
> the larger white world (of family, friends,
> employees, etc., who do not live in inter-
> racial communities) may conclude that for
> him such a community is a step down.[3]

Table 7 presents the responses of the statisti-
cally relevant subgroups in the sample. As expected
from a consideration of the general results, a

TABLE 7

Attitudes Toward Racial Integration
(In Percent)

Subgroups of Low- and Moderate- Income Interviewees	Prefer Segregation	Prefer Integration	Total
Low-Income White-- No Husband	33	67	100
Low-Income White-- Husband	64	36	100
Low-Income Black-- No Husband	33	67	100
Low-Income Black-- Husband	32	68	100
Moderate-Income White--No Husband	33	67	100
Moderate-Income White--Husband	67	33	100
Moderate-Income Black--No Husband	0	100	100
Moderate-Income Black--Husband	12	88	100

majority of all the black subgroups prefer integration, but only two white subgroups contain a majority
of respondents favoring integration. Both of these
groups are white households without husbands who
may think that an integrated environment would be a
more tolerant one for them to live in.

NOTES

1.   Statement of one of the interviewees included in the sample of low- and moderate-income households.

2.   Herbert Gans, <u>The Levittowners: Ways of Life and Politics in a New Suburban Community</u> (New York: Vintage Books, 1969), p. 167.

3.   Joshua A. Fishman, "Some Social and Psychological Determinants of Intergroup Relations in Changing Neighborhoods--An Introduction to the Bridgeview Study," Presented at the sixteenth International Congress of Psychology, Bonn, Germany, August, 1960, p. 46.

3

ATTITUDES
OF SUBURBAN RESIDENTS
TO LOW
AND MODERATE
INCOME HOUSEHOLDS

"I didn't think I was prejudiced,
but you know I think I am. Isn't
that terrible?"[1]

REASON FOR STUDYING THE ATTITUDES
OF THE SUBURBANITES

The reason for studying the attitudes of suburbanities is that the suburbanites are already there,
and nobody wants them to leave. There are two aspects
to this answer. First, the negative aspect. Those
who are in the suburbs frequently have the economic
and political power to prevent construction of new
houses for low- and moderate-income households. Their
economic power is used in the marketplace to bid up
the price of land.

The most obvious manifestation of their political
power is zoning. As Richard F. Babcock, the noted
legal authority on zoning, said in his book The
Zoning Game: "Zoning has provided the device for pro-
tecting the homogeneous single-family suburb from
the city."[2] The suburban residents also have more
subtle methods at their disposal for resisting or
not providing necessary cooperation to programs that
would subsidize the construction of new homes for
low- and moderate-income families.

38   LOW AND MODERATE INCOME HOUSING

Secondly, the suburban residents have the option
of moving from their neighborhood or community if
they are sufficiently disturbed by what they perceive
to be the negative impact of housing such people.
This motivation spurred many of them, or their parents, to move to the suburbs in the first place.
Like most American cities, turn-of-the-century Dayton,
Ohio, consisted of many small, rather dense, homogeneous neighborhoods, forced together by proximity
and the sharing of some institutions and geographically constrained by the availability of public
transit and the location of work places. The automobile, the highway, and the movement of work places
from the central city have permitted the majority
of those who could afford new houses to leave the
city and move to the suburbs.

Certainly, the physical amenities that were
offered by the new houses--built on the more rural
and, initially, relatively inexpensive land of the
suburbs--did attract many of those who could afford
to pay the developer's price. However, some of
those who moved were also partly motivated by a
desire to leave older neighborhoods that were beginning to provide homes for people whose socioeconomic
and racial characteristics differed from theirs.
As the older residents moved out, the frequently
discussed pattern of neighborhood change began.
This urban evolution caused the old neighborhoods
to become homogeneous again, and the community we
call the central city wound up containing a less
affluent group of residents to support and to use
its public and private facilities and services.
On a national level, the results were demonstrated
by the 1970 census: It reported the median income
of families and unrelated individuals living in the
central cities of metropolitan areas with more than
1 million inhabitants as $7,427, while the median
income of those living outside the central city was
$10,531.[3] The Miami Valley region offers no exception
to this national situation.

Therefore, the MVRPC and the DMHA want to be
extremely careful that they do not select and implement programs that deliver new housing for low- and

moderate-income programs and, also, bring this
classic process of neighborhood change to the suburbs.
They cannot attain their goal unless the attitudes
of the suburbanites are properly discerned and considered as one step in the selection and evaluation
of alternative low- and moderate-income housing
programs.

INFORMATION SOUGHT FROM
SUBURBAN RESIDENTS

The suburban resident has chosen his present
location because it offers him the highest housing
value for which he feels he wants to pay. This
housing value includes more than physical shelter,
space, and comfort. It also includes a host of
social, environmental, and public services that are
attached to the suburban location he has chosen to
live in.

In the research conducted for this study, an
attempt was made to understand the reasons behind
this choice of a neighborhood and community. Direct
questions were asked about the kind of housing patterns the suburbanites would like to see for low-
and moderate-income families. The survey also emphasized finding out how the suburbanite felt his
neighborhood would be affected by the various type
of households brought to his neighborhood or community
(by the successful implementation of the programs
that this study evaluates).

The survey also probed for the reasons behind
the feelings of the suburbanite--what did the suburbanite associate with the provision of low- and
moderate-income housing that he felt would harm his
neighborhood? Finally, programs were posed that
contained facilitating provisions aimed at allevi-
ating these objections, while also providing low-
and moderate-income housing. Thus, the suburbanite
was asked to reevaluate his initial objections,
given the availability of a comprehensive program
aimed at eliminating some of the objections frequently raised by his group.

Interviews of approximately thirty-five minutes
were conducted with 288 respondents at their places
of residence. The survey coincided with the MVRPC's
release of its study, A Housing Plan for the Miami
Valley Region. This study allocated a percent of
low- and moderate-income households to each of fifty-
three planning units or subareas of the region.*
This report attracted a great deal of regionwide
publicity. Many respondents referred to the proposed
housing allocations during their interview. It is
believed by us that this study highlighted the possibility that some low- and moderate-income households
would be placed in their community and that this
knowledge tended to promote honest reactions to the
prospect. A copy of the questionnaire used to guide
the interviews is attached (see Appendix B).

THE SAMPLE

Despite the many cliches to the contrary, there
is no such thing as a "typical suburb." There are,
in fact, numerous typical suburbs. To understand
the makeup of a specific suburb, at a minimum, class
and mobility factors must be taken into consideration.
For example, suburbs may be classified as either
terminal or nonterminal. The inhabitants of the former
generally view their home as their last house, while
residents of nonterminal suburbs anticipate moving
as they have job promotions. Either type of suburb
may be inhabited by primarily upper middle-class
professional/administrative/managerial households,
middle-class white collar families, or lower middle-
class blue collar or working class families. The
working class household, however, is most often found
in a terminal suburb, since its upward mobility is
often occupationally constrained.

Four Miami Valley suburban communities were
chosen for the survey because each appeared to be

---

*The MVRPC study was released in July, 1970.
The interviews for this study were conducted during
July and August of 1970.

a distinct regional prototype. The first developed
its character as a small city surrounded by farmland,
outside the main metropolitan county. It has a number
of apartment units, as well as single-family homes.
It has the lowest median family income of all four
areas, as well as the lowest median house value.
This community has a substantial black population
and is, also, the location of a recently completed
federally assisted housing project.

Area 2, though within the county, is geographically further from the center city than the other
two. It is a fairly prosperous and rapidly growing
community, virtually all white, and desirous of
maintaining a suburban, low-density residential
environment. Its population consists primarily of
middle and working class households.

Area 3, a growing suburb, with a number of
apartment complexes as well as single-family homes,
is the richest of the surveyed communities. It is
an all-white area, with the highest family income
and house value of the four areas, as well as the
highest percent of sound housing units. A visual
inspection of the houses and yards of the community
identifies area 3 as an upper middle-income suburb.
Despite resistance, particularly in Area 2, both
areas 2 and 3 are attracting an increasing number
of multifamily residences.

Area 4 is a black suburban area. It is virtually all single-family and attracts the more well-
to-do black families who can afford to move from
the center city. It is directly adjacent to the
larger city, but still provides an essentially
suburban living environment. A more complete
description of sampling methodology can be found in
Appendix C.

The original sample design was to include half
single, half multifamily households. The obtained
proportion was 59 percent single families and 41
percent apartment dwellers. Apartment households
were more difficult to interview, because they
generally spend less time in their residences--

tending not to be in the child-rearing stage of
life--and generally were less motivated to partici-
pate. Thus, interviews were conducted on the week-
ends and until 8 P.M.; in addition, telephone
appointments were made whenever possible with the
most hard-to-reach residents.

More significant and difficult to overcome was
the problem of motivating the upper-income (over
$25,000) apartment dwellers to grant interviews.
Many of these residents were indifferent to the
prospect of placing low-income households in the
suburbs. Like the private home dwellers of equivalent income, they felt their privacy adequately
protected by the building and management and, in the
main, they were correct. As one apartment building
manager put it when he refused permission to interview his tenants: "We don't even let the Girl Scouts
in to sell cookies." Then, too, these residents
were willing to move if the management ceased to
provide a satisfactory level of privacy and safety.

The initial sample design specified three major
income categories: $10,000-$15,000, $16,000-$24,000,
and $25,000 and over. Households below $10,000 were
omitted because they could technically be defined as
moderate-income families, according to the categorization used to select the low-/moderate-income
sample. House value or apartment rent was used as
a substitute for household income. The obtained
sample reflected the imperfect correlation between
housing cost and income. Thus, 15 percent of the
surveyed households had incomes of less than $10,000,
24 percent between $10,000-$15,000, 28 percent between
$15,000-$25,000, and 21 percent above $25,000;
12 percent did not answer the question.

One-third of all the suburban households
surveyed contained two or more adult wage earners.
Two-thirds of the second wage earners worked full
time, and one-third part time. Of all households
surveyed, 55 percent of the heads were employed in
managerial, administrative, professional, or technical occupations. Ten percent worked in white
collar jobs or sales; 9 percent were blue collar

or service workers; 6 percent were self-employed;
2 percent served in the military; and 9 percent were
retired. The remaining 3 percent were accounted for
by student household heads, families with no head
of household, and those who refused to answer the
question.

The majority of the sample head of households
were college-educated persons under the age of forty-
five. Fifty-seven percent of all family heads were
over thirty, and 14 percent were over sixty-one.
Twenty-four percent of all household heads were not
high school graduates; 19 percent attended one to
three years of college or a technical, vocational,
or business school; 28 percent were college graduates;
and an equal percentage had received postgraduate
training.

We also asked the head of household's voting
status: 39 percent were registered Republicans,
19 percent registered Democrats, and 11 percent
registered Independents. Twenty-two percent were
not registered; 1 percent were not U.S. citizens;
and the remaining 6 percent refused to answer.

WHAT THE SUBURBANITES LIKE
ABOUT THEIR SUBURBS

The majority of those surveyed had lived at
their present address one to five years. Only 2
percent expected to move within the coming year, and
half of these intended to remain in the Miami Valley
region.

Each respondent was asked to specify the major
factors influencing selection of his or her present
home. The question was open-ended but, subsequently,
categorized into accessibility, social, and factors
directly associated with house or apartment. Thirty-
four percent cited proximity to work, friends,
schools, or other institutions; 32 percent mentioned
factors associated with the social makeup of the
neighborhood. Familiarity with the neighborhood,
the prestige or exclusiveness of the area, and the

type of people living at the location were the most
frequently specified social "locational" factors.
The remaining 24 percent identified features of the
house/apartment as being highly influential in their
housing choice. Sixteen percent of the total sample
stated that the school system was what drew them to
their present location. Some respondents indicated
that all these factors were important.

OBSERVATIONS ON SOCIAL FACTORS
AND SOCIAL CLASS

The importance placed by the suburbanite on
social factors as reasons behind the selection and
continued satisfaction with a suburban location will
not surprise those familiar with the research that
has been done in other suburbs. They would recognize
also that the suburbanite's desire for similar social
environments and his attitude toward his home and
neighborhood cannot be understood without recognizing
the existence and importance of the social class
concept.

Since the United States has never known a feudal
period or a landed aristocracy, we have not been
sympathetic to the concept of class. However, out
of familiar everyday American conversations comes
out the recognition of class differences. In his
book, Class in Suburbia, William M. Dobriner points
out this historic American paradox: "Thus, while
they do not consciously think in terms of class, do
they nevertheless act as if class relations were a
central and significant part of their lives."[4]

This conflict between thought and deed is particularly prevalent with the middle class. In fact,
the concept that "class is of no consequence" is an
indication of membership in the middle class. The
upper- and lower-class belief systems are much more
sympathetic to the class concept. John R. Seeley
points out that the concept of classlessness is not
only inherent in middle-class life, but also tends
to perpetuate itself in the selection of intimate
relationships, including marriage partners. He
continues:

But people who think along these lines
are predominantly middle class people
and the contrary views (on different
ground) of the lower and upper classes
tend to render their possessors repug-
nant or less attractive as possible
partners for intimacy or marriage.
The very belief, therefore, that 'class
is of no consequence' (which is on one
side a middle-class view exclusively)
becomes a token of compatibility and a
basis for intimacy and insofar as it
determines friendship, membership in a
clique, and marriage, a potent factor
in the maintenance of the class bound-
aries which 'do not exist,' 'do not
matter,' or 'ought not to be considered.'5

When one recognizes that the failure to accept
the existence of class status differences even
influences the middle-class marriage decisions, it
is not difficult to see why the importance of this
social factor in the suburbs is often obscured.
Nevertheless, while the physical features of a
house or apartment are important to the residents,
they are buying much more than the shelter and
physical comfort it provides. Seeley discussed the
relationship between social or class status and the
physical dwelling unit in his book, which described
the lives and motivations of upper middle-class
terminal suburbanites.

Property is an essential component of
status in Crestwood Heights. The
Crestwooder who owns an adequate house
has become a substantial member of the
community and, as such, is respected
and admired by his peers. The house
and its furnishings, the street and
the street number; the location in
Crestwood--all are acquired items
which make up the total property complex of the house.

It is on these items, and other
similar ones, that the competitive struggle of the Crestwooder for power focuses.
These are the symbols around which he
must center his efforts to realize the
'good life' and organize the strivings
which lend a meaning to his existence.
Property does not, then, acquire its
value directly from its intrinsic monetary worth, or from narrow utilitarian
considerations, but from the public
evaluations of things as they evolve in
the markets of exchange and in the ri-
alto of status. It is the attributes
imputed to broadloom, or a particular
style of architecture, or the work of a
fashionable artist, or a street and a
number, which gives them an edge as
weapons wielded in the battle for
social position. Utility is secondary
to social acceptability.[6]

Clearly, then, a house is far more than shelter.
Its location in terms of its social milieu often
outweighs the importance of its size or quality.
To the outside world, and, more important, to the
hidden psyche of the owner, his house serves as the
material definition of his status. Furthermore, it
helps define the future position of his children,
since such status is transferable, particularly in
its ability to provide proximate socially acceptable
associates, friends, and potential marital partners.
However, in this study, we found the social and
physical aspects of housing satisfaction to be
tightly linked. A well-maintained house and yard
were valued for themselves and as signs of the
neighborhood's social status. This conclusion was
also suggested by a recently completed study by the
University of Michigan Institute for Social Research,
which researched people's responses to residential
environments that differ in the extent to which they
are planned. It states: "Whether a neighborhood is
'well kept up' is the best single prediction of
neighborhood satisfaction. The compatibility of
neighborhood residents is the next most important
factor."[7]

REACTIONS TO ALTERNATIVE
HOUSING STRUCTURES

Each of the suburbanites we interviewed was shown the same eight photographs of housing structures that were shown to the low-/and moderate-income central city residents sampled (see Chapter 2). However, the suburbanites were asked a series of questions aimed at finding out how they would respond to these structures if others lived in them, rather than determining which they preferred for themselves.

First, each suburban respondent was shown the eight photographs, one at a time, and asked to assume it would be inhabited by the type of people currently living in his neighborhood. The sample suburbanites were asked to specify how they believed each structure would (a) affect their neighborhood and (b) affect their community. They were asked to record their attitudes by selecting from a response on a five-point scale, with one being the most beneficial, five the most harmful, and three indicating a neutral response. Had time permitted, we would have tried more carefully to control for landscaping, the angle of the shot, and other factors, which may, to a greater or lesser extent, affect the viewer.

Many suburban respondents thought Structure 1 cheap and motel-like. Conversely, the low- and moderate-income sample selected this structure as their most preferred multifamily unit and enjoyed its uncluttered lines; they believed they would feel at home and comfortable in such a dwelling. Structure 2 did not elicit extreme reactions from either sample: it was neither liked nor disliked to any great degree.

Structure 3 was the only presentation of a high rise. This eleven-story building triggered almost uniformly hostile feelings among the low-/moderate-income sample. While many suburbanites also rejected the construction of any high-rise structure in their neighborhood, a small minority thought it to be quite attractive and a welcome addition if located else-where in their community.

The suburban sample was attracted to what they viewed as warm tones and Spanish design of structure 4 and felt, for the most part, that it would fit in well with their community. The low-/moderate-income sample selected structure 4 to be their second most preferred multifamily unit.

Structure 6, the brick and frame building, was selected by both the low-/moderate-income and suburban respondents as their second choice of single-family house. Because similar structures are found throughout the region, this could not be singled out as a residence of subsidized households. On the other hand, structure 5 was perceived by both samples as quite ordinary.

Structure 7 is a modern wood frame residence-- the only modern option in this survey. As previously noted, the picture does not show the complete structure, which may account for some of the nega- tive reaction to it. The suburban sample was pola- rized in its opinion of the house: some respondents were attracted and others repelled. The low-/ moderate-income households throughly disliked the picture.

Structure 8, a brick house with white shutters and trim, was the overall favorite of the majority of all respondents. The Miami Valley suburb contains numerous versions of this structure, which has traditional appeal in the Midwest.

Since the suburbanites were asked to specify how they felt about each building by selecting from a five-point scale, it was possible to give each of the structures a score based on their responses. Table 8 presents these scores for the eight buildings under the two locational situations that we posed.

Structures 4, 6, and 8 are perceived to have a potentially neutral impact upon their neighborhood, while 1, 3, 5, and 7 are felt to be harmful. All eight structures are believed to have a neutral impact if located elsewhere in the community.

TABLE 8

Suburban Reactions to Housing Structures

Structure	Locational Situation	Average Score*
Apartment 1	Neighborhood	3.76
	Community	3.17
Apartment 2	Neighborhood	3.57
	Community	2.96
Apartment 3	Neighborhood	3.90
	Community	3.28
Apartment 4	Neighborhood	3.32
	Community	2.87
House 5	Neighborhood	3.71
	Community	2.55
House 6	Neighborhood	3.33
	Community	2.90
House 7	Neighborhood	3.64
	Community	3.22
House 8	Neighborhood	3.16
	Community	2.78

*Average score definitions: 1.00-2.49 equal Positive; 2.50-3.50 equal Neutral; and 3.51-5.00 equal Negative.

Each respondent was also asked to pick the structures he or she would least like to see located in their neighborhood or community. Table 9 gives the results obtained after asking this question. Houses 5 and 7 and apartments 3 and 1 were most frequently cited as the most disliked. However, the respondents were always less vehement about their dislikes when asked about the buildings being located in the community, but not in their neighborhood.

Each respondent was then asked why he or she thought the three most disliked structures would be harmful to the neighborhood or community. Table 10 summarizes the respondents' reactions to this question. More than a half felt the fact that "the structure wouldn't fit in well with this area" to be a "very important" reason. Other primary factors are the structure's personal unattractiveness to them and the fear that such structures would have an adverse effect on property values. Reasons associated with apartment buildings were in the main considered to be less important. Factors written in as "other" are always considered to be very important to the respondents; otherwise, they would not have been introduced. Fifteen respondents specified that their neighborhood needs better buildings. However, this is simply a stronger restatement of the opinion that

TABLE 9

Least-Liked Structures
(In Percent)

Picture Number	Dislike
5	23
3	21
1	19
7	15
2	9
4	5
6	4
8	3

the structure would not fit in well with the area.
A few respondents were opposed to apartments on the
grounds that they encouraged too high a density and
traffic problems. Only two respondents openly stated
opposition to the structures on the grounds that they
would attract the wrong kind of element to their
area. However, when one considers these responses
in conjunction with expressed attitudes toward individuals of lower economic status, one is led to
suggest that this was an implicit motivation underlying some of the other responses.

SUBURBAN RESPONSES TO PROSPECT OF LOW AND MODERATE INCOME HOUSEHOLDS IN THEIR COMMUNITY

The interviewers made the following statement
to each of the suburbanites in the sample:

> Although there is a tendency to lump
> all low and moderate housing assistance
> programs together, in actuality both
> the type of structures and type of
> households residing in that structure
> frequently differ. In addition to the
> above complexities, you may feel that
> a certain percent of each of these
> groups is a positive factor, while
> another percentage would exert either a
> neutral or negative influence on your
> neighborhood or community. We would
> like to have your reactions to the pro-
> vision of housing of the following
> percent levels and for the following
> household types, if this housing were
> to be constructed somewhere within
> your neighborhood.

The following choices were posed for each of
twelve low- and moderate-income household types
postulated as being introduced into the neighborhood
population at a 5 percent, 10 percent, and 20 percent
level: It would--

TABLE 10

Reasons Given for Feeling that Structures
Would Harm the Neighborhood or Community
(In Percent)

	Very Important	Important	Unimportant	No Answer
The structure is unattractive to me.	43	45	10	2
The structure wouldn't fit in well with this area.	52	39	7	2
Property values would decline if such structures were to be built here.	43	38	17	2
Apartment units will lower the status of the neighborhood.	27	34	35	3
Apartment buildings overtax such community services as water, sewage, police or fire.	23	31	41	4
Apartment buildings overtax the community school system.	31	27	39	3
Other (specify):				
Neighborhood needs better buildings.	15			
Structures are too small.	3			
Structures won't be maintained.	3			
Apartments promote too high a density.	2			
Apartments promote traffic problems.	2			
Structures attract wrong element.	2			

1. Greatly improve the neighborhood.
2. Improve the neighborhood.
3. Allow the neighborhood to remain
   the same.
4. Harm the neighborhood somewhat.
5. Harm the neighborhood greatly.

This system permitted us to use the survey results and calculate average or mean scores for each of the low- and moderate-income household groups at each of three levels of introduction as a part of the neighborhood (see Table 11). As these averages approach one, the perceived impact of the low- and moderate-income group upon the suburbanites who perceive them as potential neighbors is strongly positive. Conversely, a score near five would indicate that the low- and moderate-income group is generally considered to have a very harmful effect upon the suburban neighborhood. The following is a guide for evaluating these average scores:

| | Nature of Response to Low- and Moderate- |
Mean Scores	Income Groups
1.00-2.49	Positive
2.50-3.50	Neutral
3.51-5.00	Negative

When the new group was postulated as making up 20 percent of the neighborhood's population, all but the moderate-income white households with husbands were regarded as being very harmful to the neighborhood. When the new group was only to make up 10 percent of the neighborhood, the group of moderate-income white households with no husbands falls out of the negative into the neutral response category.

When it was postulated that the low- and moderate-income groups would constitute only 5 percent of the neighborhood population, the following groups were also considered to have a neutral effect: low-income white households with husbands, moderate-income black households with husbands, and moderate-income black households with no husbands.

TABLE 11

Suburban Reactions to Low-/Moderate-Income Groups

| | Proportion of Total Population | | |
Type of New Residents	5 Percent Average Score*	10 Percent Average Score*	20 Percent Average Score*
Low-Income White--Elderly	3.23	3.57	3.94
Low-Income Black--Elderly	3.55	3.88	4.20
Low-Income White--Physically Handicapped	3.33	3.59	3.90
Low-Income Black--Physically Handicapped	3.57	3.86	4.15
Low-Income White Family--Husband	3.46	3.77	3.98
Low-Income White Family--No Husband	3.64	3.98	4.29
Low-Income Black Family--Husband	3.67	3.64	4.30
Low-Income Black Family--No Husband	3.91	4.16	4.38
Moderate-Income White Family--Husband	3.07	3.19	3.37
Moderate-Income White Family-- No Husband	3.19	3.32	3.64
Moderate-Income Black Family--Husband	3.31	3.51	3.75
Moderate-Income Black Family-- No Husband	3.53	3.77	4.01

*Average score definitions: 1.00-2.49 equal positive; 2.50-3.50 equal neutral; and 3.51-5.00 equal negative.

The low-income white family without a husband and all
low-income black families were believed to be potentially harmful, even if they were to constitute only
5 percent of the neighborhood's resident population.

In addition to calculating the results obtained
from the total sample of suburbanites, we also broke
out the responses received in each of the four areas
and calculated separate average scores derived from
each. These averages did not differ significantly
from each other except in one case: The moderate-
income black family with no husband is perceived as
a neutral addition to neighborhoods in areas 2 and 3
if they make up 5 percent of the population, while
areas 1 and 4 perceive them as negative, even at
this relatively low proportion.

The similarity of responses between the four
areas was startling. Therefore, even though we had
not originally planned to subdivide the suburbanite
sample further, we did break it up into twelve subgroups to ascertain if attitudes toward low-moderate-
income households were highly dependent upon a set
of mutually exclusive demographic factors, which
include income, age, the presence of children, and
whether the respondent household lived in a single-
family house or a multifamily dwelling. (A complete
description of these mutually exclusive categories
can be found in Appendix D.)*

The responses of each suburban household category to the eight most prevalent low- and moderate-
income subgroups were totaled--that is, to low- and
moderate-income households subdivided by race and
whether or not there was a husband in the household.
A separate score was calculated for each of the twelve
suburban subgroups' responses to each of the eight
low-income groups postulated as making up 5 percent,
10 percent, and 20 percent of the neighborhood

---

*The tables and text will ignore the existence
of children, since it is subsumed in the multifamily;
single-family scale.

population. The scores emanating from each subgroup
were calculated in the same manner as those that had
been previously calculated for the sample as a whole
and are shown in Table 11. The statistical relia-
bility of these scores is not as great as those shown
previously and derived from the responses of the
total sample, because of the small size of some
subgroups.* Therefore, it is much more difficult to
state firm conclusions, but some further generalizations and hypotheses seem to be indicated.

First, there are no really dramatic subgroup
divergencies from the attitudes expressed by the
suburbanite sample as a whole. None of the suburban
subgroups gave responses indicating that they considered that any of the low- and moderate-income
household groups would greatly benefit the neighborhood. Instead, all their average responses fell into
either the neutral or negative response categories.
Table 12 shows the pattern of neutral scores. Negative
scores were calculated for all the cells left blank
in Table 12. Out of the 288 responses of all suburban
subgroups to all calculated low- and moderate-income
subgroups, only the 97 indicated with an equal sign
received an average score that we defined as neutral.
The moderate-income subgroups postulated as entering
the neighborhoods received 79 of the 99 neutral
response scores. Sixty-eight white low- and moderate-
income groups postulated as living in the neighborhoods
at differing rates received neutral response scores,
while 31 black subgroups received neutral response
scores. Households with husbands were more likely
to be considered as not altering the neighborhood
than were households without husbands, and lower proportions of the low- and moderate-income households
in the neighborhood were almost universally more
popular than higher levels.

———————————

*The scores calculated for the responses of the
twelve suburban subgroups are shown in Appendix D,
along with the size of each subgroup and standard
error calculations.

TABLE 12

Neutral Scores of Suburban Responses to
Low- and Moderate-Income Groups*

(a)
Living in Single-Family Dwellings

Household Income	Age of Head of Household	Low-Income White--Husband Percent			Low-Income White--No Husband Percent			Low-Income Black--Husband Percent			Low-Income Black--No Husband Percent			Moderate-Income White--Husband Percent			Moderate-Income White--No Husband Percent			Moderate-Income Black--Husband Percent			Moderate-Income Black--No Husband Percent		
		5	10	20	5	10	20	5	10	20	5	10	20	5	10	20	5	10	20	5	10	20	5	10	20
$25,000+	Over 45													=	=	=	=								
$25,000+	Under 45	=			=						=			=	=		=	=		=	=		=		
$16,000-$24,000	Over 45	=			=			=						=	=		=	=	=	=			=		
$16,000-$24,000	Under 45													=	=		=			=					
$15,000 and Under	Over 45				=									=	=		=	=		=	=				
$15,000 and Under	Under 45	=			=			=						=	=		=	=	=	=	=		=		

(b)
Living in Multifamily Dwellings

Household Income	Age of Head of Household	Low-Income White--Husband			Low-Income White--No Husband			Low-Income Black--Husband			Low-Income Black--No Husband			Moderate-Income White--Husband			Moderate-Income White--No Husband			Moderate-Income Black--Husband			Moderate-Income Black--No Husband		
$25,000+	Over 45													=	=	=	=	=		=					
$25,000+	Under 45	=	=		=			=			=			=	=		=	=	=	=	=		=	=	=
$16,000-$24,000	Over 45													=	=					=					
$16,000-$24,000	Under 45	=												=	=	=	=	=		=					
$15,000 and Under	Over 45	=	=		=									=	=		=			=			=		
$15,000 and Under	Under 45	=												=	=	=	=	=		=	=	=	=		

*Score between 2.50 and 3.50.

Note: All blanks reflect negative scores; equal signs denote neutral scores.

57

TABLE 13

Least-Preferred Lower-Income Households
(In Percent)

Household Type	Households Listed Among the Four Least-Liked Groups
Low-Income Black--No Husband	96
Low-Income Black--Husband	69
Low-Income White--No Husband	66
Low-Income White--Husband	35
Low-Income Black--Elderly	31
Moderate-Income Black--No Husband	30
Low-Income Black--Physically Handicapped	25
Low-Income White--Physically Handicapped	12
Low-Income White--Elderly	9
Moderate-Income White--No Husband	9
Moderate-Income Black--Husband	8
Moderate-Income White--Husband	2

Table 13 presents a similar picture. It is a
compilation of the responses given to a question
asked of all the suburban interviewees who had given
three or more negative responses to the separately
postulated low-income groups under the assumption
that they would make up only 5 percent of the neighborhood population. These interviewees were asked :
Which four household types would you least like living
in your neighborhood or community? Table 13 indicates
the percent by which each of the low- and moderate
income groups was cited by the respondents.

The survey brought into the open the previously
discussed conflict between the middle-class ideal
that "everyone is equally acceptable" and the attitude
that those who differ, particularly lower-income
blacks, may be harmful to the middle-class neighborhood. Some respondents were aware of the conflicting
feelings; hence, the title of this chapter. However,
many were not aware of any inconsistency in attitude.
For example, a man stated: "I don't care what kind
of structure, even if it's next door to me, but I
don't want people who give all-night parties or
receive welfare checks." A young housewife commented:
"It would be beneficial for my daughter to live with
all kinds of people as long as they had the same ideals
and were neat and clean."

Biases toward specific lower-income subgroups
were exposed by the survey, often instituting a
personal reevaluation of beliefs and attitudes on
the part of the respondent. For example, negative
responses to the aged frequently provoked guilt
feelings, illustrated by apologetic statements, such
as: "I really get along with my parents but . . . "
Some claimed their opposition to the elderly and
physically handicapped lay in the supposition that
these groups would be unable to maintain their property. Others said that older persons are more difficult to get along with and that they are likely to
be reactionary in terms of passing school bond issues,
and so forth. All these vocalized reasons may be
less important than our culture's general antipathy
to the aged, with the concomitant psychological factor
that few Americans like being reminded of their own
advancing years.

   Families without fathers were the most harshly
condemned. The disciplining of children, and hence,
the prevention of deliquency, were considered dependent upon having a man in the house. The value
structure of the suburbanites was particularly threatened by the specter of having women with illegitimate
children living in their midst.

   The Miami Valley suburbanites show a strong
racial bias: In almost every instance, the black
household with husband was less acceptable than the
white household without. The sole exception is
that the "moderate-income black household with husband"
is slightly more acceptable than the "lower-income
white household with husband."

   Table 14 lists the number of the ninety-nine
neutral responses that we accounted for by regrouping
the respondents on the basis of age, income, and type
of residence. Suburban subgroups differed in their
reactions to the low- and moderate-income household

TABLE 14

Number of Neutral Average
Response Scores

When Suburbanites Grouped by	Number
Age of Head of Household :	
Over 45	38
Under 45	61
Total	99
Household Income:	
$25,000 and Over	37
$16,000-$24,000	24
$15,000 and Under	38
Total	99
Residence :	
Single-Family House	47
Multifamily Dwelling	52
Total	99

groups. If we break the suburbanite sample into two
age categories, we find that the young tend to be less
fearful of the impact of low- and moderate-income
households on their neighborhoods. When broken down
by income, the highest and lowest suburban income
groupings are the most generous in their evaluation
of the effect of low- and moderate-income households
will have on their neighborhood. Those living in
multiunit dwellings also appear less threatened by
the prospect.

     In spite of the generalization suggested by the
data in Table 12, a glance at Table 14 suggests that
the two least accepting suburban prototypes are the
single-family with incomes in excess of $25,000 whose
household head is over forty-five and the multifamily
household with $16,000-$24,000 household incomes and
household heads over forty-five. Thus, our generalizations about the likely tolerances of households
with higher incomes and who reside in apartments
must be used carefully.

     The most accepting household group is the one
whose head is under forty-five years of age, living
in an apartment, with household income exceeding
$25,000. However, the other unusually tolerant groups
are the single-family, under $15,000, under forty-
five, and the single-family, $16,000-$24,000, over
forty-five. While a variety of hypotheses are suggested by this data as to the groups most likely to
be tolerant of low- and moderate-income families
moving into their neighborhoods, further analysis of
the data and additional interviews are needed before
any final judgments can be reliably made.

                INHIBITORS TO HOUSING LOW AND
                  MODERATE INCOME GROUPS
                      IN THE SUBURBS

     The researchers were interested in ascertaining
the overt reasons why these low-/moderate-income groups
were perceived as threatening. Therefore, each
respondent was asked to indicate the importance of
reasons frequently given for objecting to the provision

of low-income housing in higher-income communities.
The questionnaire postulated ten statements.

These statements tested the importance the
suburbanites attached to the prospect of a drop in
property values, a decrease in housing maintenance,
a property tax increase resulting from an increase
in service needs, a drop in the quality of schools,
a decrease in the degree of neighborhood organization
resulting from an increase in crime and delinquency,
a decrease in the neighborhood's social status, and
a reduction in the neighborhood's stability. The
latter concept was introduced directly by the statement that the "neighborhood would become less stable"
and indirectly by the statements that "those people
would not fit in with the rest of the community" and
"these people would be a bad influence on my family
because they don't believe the same things we do."

The respondent was also encouraged to specify
any other reasons for his belief that these households
would be harmful to his neighborhood. Table 15 lists
the results of this part of the survey. Housing
maintenance and property values were cited as very
important motivations for more than a half of all
suburbanites interviewed. Law and order and the
stability of the neighborhood rank next highest in
importance.*

----

*Scott Donaldson, The Suburban Myth (New York:
Columbia University Press, 1969), p. 71. Maintaining
one's home, particularly the front yard, has become
both a symptom and symbol of suburban living. As one
area 3 resident so eloquently put it: "We don't cut
our grass--we manicure our lawn." Donaldson, in op.
cit, describes this phenomenon as the

        sacrosanct strip of greenery facing
        squarely toward the street and performs
        no function other than decoration.
        Suburbanites do not put up 'keep off
        the grass' signs because there is no
        need; visitors who have their own deco-
        rative greens know automatically that

Although a drop in quality of schools ranks fifth
in the "very important" category in Table 15, it must
be remembered that the first four factors affect
households without children, as well as families.
Thus, for those with children, schools were very
important. Previous research suggests that the
middle- and upper middle-class parent views the school
as the prime institutional transmitter of class
mobility. Seeley notes that in, contemporary upper
middle-class society, the school has replaced the
functions of the church.*

Thirty-one percent of the suburbanite sample
felt a drop in the neighborhood's social status to be

-----

the front lawn is to look at, not to
step on. Dogs are less cultivated;
they may relieve themselves on a neighbor's front lawn and, when they do,
they create a real community crisis
that is invariably resolved by passage
of a leashing law to keep the dogs
like the people in the homes, under
strict control.

*John R. Secley, R. Alexander Sim, and Elizabeth
Loosley; Crestwood Heights: A Study of the Culture
of Suburban Life (New York: John Wiley & Sons, Inc.,
1963), p. 400.

It is not by accident that Crestwood
Heights has literally grown up around
a school. This development has the same
social logic as had the cathedral-
centered communities of medieval
Europe, or the chapel governed towns
of seventeenth century New England.
There could be no better indication
that this central focus in the school
that a great cultural shift has
occured towards a society most of
whose dominant concerns are now secular.

TABLE 15

Reasons for Considering Low-/Moderate-
Income Households Undesirable Neighbors
(In Percent)

Reasons	Very Important	Important	Un-important	No Answer
Property values would drop.	55	29	9	7
Property taxes would increase due to need for increased services.	36	31	26	7
Neighborhood would face a drop in social status.	31	32	30	7
Neighborhood would become less stable.	40	43	9	7
Those people would not fit in with rest of community.	29	37	25	8
Housing maintenance and conditions would decrease.	59	23	9	8
Decrease in law and order.	43	30	20	7
Change in character of neighborhood with shopping facilities catering to new groups' needs.	19	34	40	7
Drop in quality of schools.	38	18	40	7
These people would be a bad influence on my family because they don't believe the same thing we do.	15	23	54	8
Other:				
Race.	2			
Low-income persons would feel insecure in higher income areas.	1			
Low-income households have too many children.	1			

a very important factor in their rejection of low-
and moderate-income households as neighbors, while
30 percent of the sample considered it to be unimportant. This factor was considered far more important
to those households living in areas with relatively
high social status, while those respondents living
in less prestigious suburban communities indicated
they did not feel they had as much to lose. Thus,
the factor of social status serves as an inhibitor
for specific suburbs, while such factors as property
values, maintenance, neighborhood stability, and law
and order affect a significant proportion of residents
in all communities.

The possibility of households with substantially
less income moving into their neighborhoods or communities threatens many higher-income suburbanites.
They fear that the provision of housing for other
presently excluded central city residents will lower
the social, physical, and public service benefits
they now enjoy and, simultaneously, cause property
to drop in monetary value. Thus, one would think
that programs to alleviate these inhibiting impacts
would serve to facilitate the acceptance of lower-
and moderate-income housing in suburban middle- and
upper middle-income neighborhoods. The next chapter
reports on our attempts to test this hypothesis.

                            NOTES

1. Direct quote from a suburban interviewee.

2. Richard F. Babcock, The Zoning Game (Madison,
Milwaukee, and London: The University of Wisconsin
Press, 1969), p. 3.

3. U.S. Bureau of the Census, Current Population
Reports, "Income in 1969 of Families and Persons in
the United States" (Series P-60, No. 75) (Washington,
D.C.: U.S. Government Printing Office, 1970), Table
16, p. 32.

4. William M. Dobriner, Class In Suburbia
(Englewood Cliffs, N.J.: Prentice-Hall, Inc., 1963),
p. 34.

66   LOW AND MODERATE INCOME HOUSING

5.   John R. Seeley, R. Alexander Sim, and
Elizabeth Loosley, <u>Crestwood Heights: A Study of
the Culture of Suburban Life</u> (New York: John Wiley
& Sons, Inc., 1963), p. 400.

6.   Seeley, Sim, Loosley, <u>op</u>. <u>cit</u>., p. 46.

7.   John Lansing, Robert Morans, and Robert
Zehner, <u>Planned Residential Environments</u> (Ann Arbor:
University of Michigan, Institute for Social Research,
1970), p. x.

4

SUBURBAN RESPONSE
TO COMPREHENSIVE
HOUSING PROGRAMS
FOR LOW AND MODERATE
INCOME FAMILIES

"These people need property to give
them security and pride. The only objection I have to this housing in the
area is the decline in property values."*

ACCEPTANCE OF PROGRAMS BY SUBURBANITES
THAT IMPROVE OR SAFEGUARD THEIR COMMUNITY
WHILE PROVIDING NEW HOUSING FOR LOW
AND MODERATE INCOME HOUSEHOLDS

After getting their reactions to low- and moderate-income groups, the suburbanites were asked if
they would accept programs that improved or safeguarded
their community, while providing new housing for low-
and moderate-income households. The suburbanites
who had thought that some low- and moderate-income
household types would greatly harm their neighborhood
also told us the specific features that they thought
would be harmed. Thus, we knew which groups they
objected to and what general attitudes and specific
fears prompted these objections. This information
suggested the possibility of facilitating the acceptance of the group objected to by bringing it into
the suburbs with programs that also safeguard or

_____

*Comment of a suburban interviewee.

even improve the neighborhood and community features that the suburbanites value.

It could be said that such an expansion of housing programs is a matter of simple justice--a requirement for avoiding imposing the social costs of housing low- and moderate-income households on the suburbs. Or it might be more cynically said that such comprehensive programs are needed to bribe the suburbs into accepting their fair share of the region's less-affluent and minority households. The research program did not consider this philosophical issue; instead, the suburbanites, were surveyed to ascertain the factors that would serve to facilitate the placement of low-income house in the Dayton suburbs.

Therefore, the interviewers presented a series of five questions, each of which asked about the respondent's degree of acceptance of the privision of low- and moderate-income housing in their neighborhood if this would result in one of the following:

A. The government paying for an improved physical plant as well as increasing the quality level of the education given to the children in your community.

B. An assurance that crime and delinquency would not show any increase.

C. An assurance that the households residing in the new housing units would share your values, beliefs and attitudes toward family, work, religion and education.

D. An assurance that property values will be maintained.

E. A guaranteed increase in level of services, such as more frequent garbage collection, improved sanitation, water, fire and police protection without any increase in your property tax.

These assertions about what would accompany the housing programs were followed with the full list of

low- and moderate-income households, grouped by
demographic characteristics, and the suburbanite was
asked in each case to choose one of the following
levels of acceptance:

1. Greatly accepting
2. Moderately accepting
3. Indifferent to
4. Moderately unaccepting
5. Greatly unaccepting.

The answers to these questions are discussed
next. Because of the number of questions asked and
the complexity of the issues posed, no set level of
low- and moderate-income groups as a proportion of
the neighborhood was mentioned. However, it is
evident from the results obtained to the previous
list of questions that within any one neighborhood
that includes lower- and middle- or higher-income
households, stability will be difficult to preserve
if the low-to-moderate-income group appears to make
up a significant proportion of the population. This
factor will be discussed further in Chapter 8, but
it is mentioned here to suggest that a relatively
low level of low- and moderate-income household pene-
trations into the neighborhood (say, 5 percent) was
probably in the minds of the respondents as they
answered these questions.

These questions were made up at the conclusion
of a pretest with a smaller sample of suburban residents. If the survey were to be redone, two other
possible "facilitators" would be added to the list,
because they appeared so important in the minds of
the suburbanites--there would be a program to guarantee
property maintenance and the stipulation that the
housing provided for the low- and moderate-income
households would be owner-occupied.

SOME GOVERNMENTAL PROGRAMS
LACK CREDIBILITY

Inquiries about the acceptability of various
low-income groups if they were provided houses in

conjunction with programs that also improved or
preserved desirable neighborhood features caused a
significant number of the suburbanites to question
the question. Many of them doubted the government's
ability to implement the postulated programs, while
others expressed a bias against government--primarily
federal. One said: "I'm totally against any kind
of government control." Another stated: "I personally
don't believe all this assurance but--it sounds like
a government project--which means more taxes."

The percentage of all respondents who refused
to answer these questions because they did not think
the programs were credible or because they opposed
federal programs is listed in Table 16. The finding
that many citizens think that governmental claims
lack credibility is not too surprising, but it is
very significant. There is, also, an apparently
explainable logic to the relative credibility that
the respondents assigned to differing types of
federal programs.

Thirteen percent of the respondents did not
want governmental interference in education, even
if it meant an in-pouring of federal dollars. However, few doubted that educational quality could be
improved or preserved if the arrival of their new
low- and moderate-income families was accompanied
by the receipt of added money for the local educational system. Conversely, relatively few respondents
opposed the idea of the government attempting to
preserve or improve law and order, but 15 percent
did not believe that the government would or could
accomplish this while low- and moderate-income
families were moving in. Similarly, 20 percent
refused to believe "an assurance that the households
residing in these new housing units would share your
values, beliefs, and attitudes toward family, work,
religion, and education."

Fifteen percent of the respondents doubted the
possibility of "an assurance that property values
will be maintained." However, in spite of the fact
that such a relatively significant proportion of
the suburbanites doubted the government's ability

TABLE 16
Respondents Who Question Programs
To Improve or Preserve Valued
Neighborhood Features
(In Percent)

Programs To Accompany Low- and Moderate-Income Programs that Pre-serve or Improve Neighborhood Level of	Not Possible-- Modal*	Against Federal Programs-- Modal*
Educational Quality	3	13
Law and Order	15	3
Social Values	20	4
Property Values	15	3
Local Public Services	12	15

*The percentage of those who felt these programs could not work varied somewhat with the makeup of the low- and moderate-income groups they were being asked about. For example, the percentage of those who did not believe that programs could assure that crime and delinquency would not show any increase went to 16 percent when the respondents were asked about the acceptability of moderate-income white families without husbands under the stipulation that such a program would exist.

to protect them from market reverses, only 3 percent objected to the concept of such assurances. When it comes to promising an increased level of services without any increase in property taxes, both the credibility and the concept draw negative responses: 12 percent do not believe the promise, and 15 percent object to the idea of the federal government becoming involved in such local services.

EFFECTIVENESS OF THE "FACILITATORS"
IN GAINING SUBURBAN ACCEPTANCE

One of the most important findings of the research was that the overwhelming majority of those
who found the facilitators credible were then willing
to accept low- and moderate-income households into
their neighborhood. Since the respondents were asked
to choose between the five levels of acceptance mentioned above, it was possible to calculate average
mean scores to gauge the level of acceptance that
was associated with each program. A score of between
1.00 and 2.49 could be interpreted to mean that the
respondents were, on the average, positive to accepting
the groups. A score of between 2.50 and 3.50 would
be neutral, while a score of between 3.51 and 5.00
could be interpreted as negative. Thus, these scores
could be compared with those previously shown in
Table 11 of Chapter 3, describing the reaction of the
suburban group to the various low-/moderate-income
groups under the assumption they make up 5 percent of
the population but when no mention is made of such
facilitating programs. Table 17 permits such a com-
parison by showing these two sets of scores side-by-
side.

The inclusion of programs to preserve or enhance
the features of the neighborhood environment that
the suburbanites fear many be harmed by the low- and
moderate-income households dramatically increases the
acceptability of the incoming groups. Previously,
there had been no positive responses and six negative
responses, but with the inclusion of these provisions,
those suburbanites who find the facilitators credible
made responses that are at a minimum neutral to each
of the groups.

The two programs that did the most to induce the
acceptance of the low- and moderate-income groups by
the total suburban sample were assurances that property values will be maintained and a guaranteed
increase in level of services, such as more frequent
garbage collection, improved sanitation, water, fire
and police protection, without any increase in the
property tax.

TABLE 17

Average Response Scores when Facilitating Program Elements Are Included,
Compared to Scores Reflecting Expectations Concerning the Impact of Low-
and Moderate-Income Groups Making Up 5 Percent of the Neighborhood's
Population When No Such Program Elements Are Present

| | | Program Elements | | | | No Programs--Low-/Moderate-Income Group |
Income Groups	Educational Quality	Crime and Delinquency	Social Values	Property Values	Public Services	Makes Up 5 percent of Neighborhood
Low-Income White Family--Husband	2.6	2.5	2.4	2.3	2.3	3.46
Low-Income White Family--No Husband	2.9	2.7	n.a.	2.5	2.5	3.64
Low-Income Black Family--Husband	3.0	2.7	2.6	2.5	2.5	3.67
Low-Income Black Family--No Husband	3.3	3.0	n.a.	2.7	2.7	3.91
Moderate-Income White Family--Husband	2.6	2.4	2.3	2.2	2.2	3.07
Moderate-Income White Family--No Husband	2.8	2.6	n.a.	2.3	2.3	3.19
Moderate-Income Black Family--Husband	2.7	2.5	2.4	2.4	2.4	3.31
Moderate-Income Black Family--No Husband	3.0	2.8	n.a.	2.6	2.5	3.53
Low-Income White--Elderly	n.a.	n.a.	2.4	2.3	2.3	3.23
Low-Income Black--Elderly	n.a.	n.a.	2.6	2.5	2.4	3.55
Low-Income White--Physically Handicapped	n.a.	n.a.	2.5	2.3	2.3	3.33
Low-Income Black--Physically Handicapped	n.a.	n.a.	2.7	2.5	2.5	3.57

Note: Average mean scores--1.00-2.49 equals positive; 2.50-3.50 equals neutral; and
3.51-5.00 equals negative. N.a. indicates questions not asked because we felt programs
to alleviate were not relevant to these low- and moderate-income groups.

73

The general direction of the average responses given by the entire surveyed suburban population of 241 respondents did not vary dramatically from the averages obtained when we broke the groups' answers down by the four areas included in the survey. The only negative average response score obtained was calculated for the respondents in area 3 when asked about their acceptance of low-income black families with no husbands. Their response was negative, when posed in conjunction with facilitating the program that assured the maintenance of property values. The positive effect of the facilitator seemed to be somewhat stronger in subareas 1 and 4.

The suburban sample was also broken down into twelve subgroups discussed in the previous chapter. Correlation coefficients (R) were calculated, relating the characteristics of the suburbanites to the levels of acceptances indicated by the responses to the questions that assured the presence of the alternative facilitators.*

There was a significant correlation between the income of the respondents and the scores. Since high scores meant relatively negative acceptance levels, this suggests that the higher-income groups generally were less influenced toward accepting low- and moderate-income groups as a result of facilitating programs. A look at the scores shown in Appendix F confirms this conclusion. The scores of the less-affluent suburbanites changed more dramatically than did the reactions of suburban households earning more than $25,000. Thus, 62 percent of all the average scores that fell into the positive category were calculated for suburban subgroups with household incomes below $15,000. This result may stem partially from the fact that age in the sample correlates highly with income. Thus, the younger and more tolerant members of the sample are also likely to be least affluent. Also, it may be that those with less

_____

*The table of correlation coefficients can be found in Appendix F.

economic power are most afraid of not being able to
cope with disturbances to their housing environment
and, thus, are most accepting of offered safeguards
and cost-free improvements.

The suburban households now living in multiunit
dwellings also tended to be much more likely to accept
low- and moderate-income households, when the facilitators were postulated, than did the households in
single-family dwellings. The tendency for those
living in apartments to be less fearfull of the impact
that low- and moderate-income residents would have
on the neighborhood was referred to in Chapter 3.
This tendency is even more pronounced when the facilitating programs are postulated in conjunction with
the various low- and moderate-income groups. The
correlation between acceptance and multifamily residences is particularly great when the law and order
facilitator is offered.

The correlations between acceptance and relative
youth were also generally significant. This was particularly true when educational quality improvements
were postulated. The younger suburban households
who tended to be less fearful of the impact of low-
and moderate-income households would also probably
be the most accepting if the programs that provided
the new housing were sufficiently comprehensive to
better the neighborhood and community public facilities and services.

SUBURBAN REACTIONS TO ALTERNATIVE
TYPES OF LOW AND MODERATE
INCOME HOUSING PATTERNS

Each of the suburbanites was asked:

Which of the following two alternatives do
you most prefer, and do you prefer the
chosen alternative a great deal more, somewhat more, or just slightly more than
the other?

Alternative 1--A small number of low

and moderate income housing units built
in each neighborhood so that these households are scattered throughout the community. . . .

    Alternative 2--The low and moderate
income units to be built in a separate neighborhood within your larger community.
The neighborhood, however, would share in
the use of the community's services,
facilities and school system.

The choice the respondent was asked to make
was "forced," in that the respondent was not given
the option of opposing both alternatives and formu-
lating a third. The first alternative, which might
be labeled "scatteration," was preferred by 55
percent of the total suburbanite sample, with the
separate neighborhood concept chosen by 43 percent;
2 percent refused to answer. While the scatteration
proposal was preferred by slightly more respondents,
the gradations of responses show that those who
selected the neighborhood proposal tend to prefer it
more intensely. These gradations are presented in
Table 18.

Apartment dwellers tended to prefer a scatteration plan, while single-family households had a
decided preference for the neighborhood approach.
Judging by the latter's comments, their hope is that
such neighborhoods would be placed "somewhere else"
in the community. Many of the respondents agreed
with the housewife who felt that "low and medium
income housing should be built in one area and kept
there. It should not be distributed throughout the
better residential areas."

In selecting between these alternatives, the
single-family dwellers once again expressed their
preferences for economically and socially homogeneous
neighborhoods. However, there was a minority who
spoke up for a more diverse community, as exemplified
by the following quote: "I think neighborhoods should
be open. It's a healthy environment when there are
differences." More often, however, the acceptance

TABLE 18

Suburban Response to Alternative
Low-/Moderate-Income Housing Patterns
(In Percent)

Alternative Low-/Moderate-Income Housing Pattern	Preferring Great Deal More	Preferring Somewhat More	Preferring Slightly More	Total	Preference of Total Sample
Scatteration	49	28	23	100	55
Separate Neighborhoods	58	29	13	100	43
No Answer					2
Total					100

of less-affluent households was tempered by the tacit
or stated assumption that the neighborhood's standard
would be maintained in the upkeep of the property and
the behavior of the occupants. This attitude is
typified in the following two statements. "I wouldn't
care if someone was 109, black and crippled, just
so they would keep up the area." "I could accept
any kind of people if I was assured they would be
good people who worked hard for what they got and
took pride in that which they earned."

5

ATTITUDES
AND PERCEPTIONS
OF POLITICIANS
AND
PUBLIC OFFICIALS

"We would be glad to take care of our own poor."*

THE PUBLIC OFFICIAL SURVEY

It has become fashionable to blame all of society's ills on its politicians and public administrators. However, this study suggests that, for good or ill, such men tend to mirror the demands of their constituencies rather than set new trends.

Eighteen in-depth interviewees were drawn from a sample list of persons serving the region in one of the following public capacities: county commissioner, city manager, village or city council member, school superintendent, planning commissioner, and public housing official.

An attempt was made to include representatives from the four areas used in the suburbanite survey. Area 4 was the only area not directly represented in the political official survey, though indirectly, its residents were included in the interviews conducted with the county commissioners. Seven persons representing the city of Dayton and five from suburban

---

*The exact words of one respondent; the sentiment of many.

areas whose residents were not surveyed in this study
completed the sample.

The public official survey results, while based
on a limited number of interviews, suggest primary
generalizations, which are drawn from the uniformity
of the responses and do not appear to be dependent
on the particular role or jurisdiction of the respondent.

First, the majority of the public officials,
whether elected or appointed, are knowledgeable concerning the attitudes and preferences of their consti-
tuents--and the majority are willing to incorporate
these desires into their policy and program formula-
tions. Two respondents were attempting to circumvent
the majority's will by introducing policies that would
foment more social change than their communities
wanted. The methods of the two varied, with the first
introducing policy changes slowly and, when possible,
innocuously. The second was taking a "bull by the
horns" approach and assumed he would be looking
around for another job in the next two to four years.

Second, as the subtitle of this chapter suggests,
most of the public official respondents were willing
to encourage those housing programs which would take
care of the low- and moderate-income households within
their communities. They were quite adverse to facilitating plans that would encourage lower-income households living elsewhere in the region to migrate into
their communities. This method of looking at the
problem results in the public officials' willingness
to take care of their own elderly but their strong
opposition to accepting central city and aid to dependent children households. This complete aversion to
households without the husband-father as head lead
many respondents to stipulate the precondition that
all low- and moderate-income households moving into
their communities must share the same middle-class
values held by the present residents.

Third, there was uniform agreement that programs
which encourage ownership were better than those subsidizing renter households. The difference between

apartment or single-family house was less important
to the public official than the ownership-renter
status of the household. Ownership, in the minds of
the public officials, is equated with responsibility,
while renters are considered to be less desirable
citizens.

Fourth, many felt that there should be a way to
assure the local communities that all new low and
moderate income housing projects would blend in with
the local architecture. Several suggested an architectural review board as the appropriate mechanism
to assure that the new low/moderate income projects
would meet the communities' design specifications.

Fifth, many felt it important to separate the
school issue from the problem of providing low/mod-
erate-income housing. One respondent suggested that
property taxes should be distributed between communities, so that the richer community with fewer children
would not be benefited more than the poorer community
with more children. Property taxes would be redis-
tributed according to the number of children in the
local school district. A few discussed the unfair-
ness of public housing projects not paying their com-
mensurate share of school taxes. Still others felt
that the introduction of low-income households would
not only overburden their school system but would
reduce the extra middle-class benefits that were
already in short supply, such as the volunteer mothers
to serve as community leaders, Boy Scout and Girl
Scout leaders, and P.T.A. members.

Three other points of view expressed by a minority
of the respondents and reflect the interviewees'
specific role. While these are not majority opinions,
they are important in that they help identify problem
areas, which should not be ignored in any regional
housing program.

First, federal public housing guidelines were
viewed as unnecessarily complex, with too much red
tape retarding the provision of new dwelling units
in the region. There was also opposition to not
giving the tenants more of a choice as to where they

would live. (If a tenant should refuse an offered
unit three times in a row, even if this unit were in
the same structure, he or she would have to be put
at the bottom of the DMHA list.)

Second, one respondent felt that the subsidization of new moderate-income households was unfair to
the working class already living in the community.
He stated that these people are struggling to keep
up with their mortgage payments and to maintain their
property, and suggested that it might be more equitable to give these existing residents the new housing
and use the houses that they vacated for the incoming
moderate-income households.

Third, the public officials representing areas
whose low land value make them the most likely location for low- and moderate-income housing are most
vocal against speeding up the use of these housing
programs. One stated that it is the residents of his
community who have already "paid the price" once by
moving from West Dayton to their present location
who are most in opposition. It is, also, these residents who have the fewest options to move again,
should large numbers of low- and moderate-income
households now come to the area.

PUBLIC OFFICIALS' REACTIONS
TO STRUCTURAL TYPES

Each public official was asked how he felt his
constituency would respond to a variety of housing
structures, which included the following types:
owner-occupied single-family house, renter-occupied
single-family house, free-standing low-rise apartments, free-standing high-rise apartments, high-rise
projects, low-rise projects, garden-type apartments,
and townhouse apartments.* He was also instructed

----

*Asking an individual to relate how others feel
about an issue is a frequently used technique in
survey research to obtain sensitive information in
an indirect way. In this survey, the technique was

not to consider the specific household type who would
be living in the structure but, rather, to react to
the structure, irrespective of who would occupy it.
If the respondent persisted in knowing the type of
people who would be living in each of the structures,
then he was told--similar to the type of people currently living in his community. The recapitulation
of this portion of the survey methodology is not
meant to infer that none of the respondents associated
the structure type with low- and moderate-income
households. It was hoped that each of them would at
least emphasize their reactions to the structure
type versus household type. Table 19 highlights some
of the region's structural preferences. The most
prominent preference is for the "owner" rather than
a renter household, irrespective of the demographic
makeup of the renter.

One public official put it very well when he
said that, to many suburbanites, anyone living in an
apartment is considered to be "somewhat immoral."
He then laughed and said he ought to ask these people:
"Were you immoral when you lived in an apartment?"
However, it is not just the apartment dweller but
the renter per se who is suspect. He is considered
to be less interested in maintaining his property and
less stable in terms of life style, and generally sus-
pected to be of a lower economic class. Thus, the
renter of a single-family home and the renter of a
garden apartment are considered to be equally acceptable in the eyes of the respondents. Townhouse
apartments are perceived to be slightly less acceptable. Low-rise apartment buildings, while less
acceptable than the preceding structural types, are
far more acceptable than a high-rise building. Housing projects are viewed as least acceptable, with
high-rise projects being virtually unacceptable to all.

At the completion of this question, all respondents were asked to state the reasons underlying any

---

being used in a straightforward manner, so that it
could be ascertained how well the public official
could read his constituency.

TABLE 19

Public Officials' Projections of Their Constituents'
Reactions to Structure Types
(In Percent)

Structure Types	Greatly Accepting	Moderately Accepting	Indifferent	Moderately Unaccepting	Greatly Unaccepting	Total*
Owner-Occupied Single-Family Houses	89	11	0	0	0	100
Renter-Occupied Single-Family Houses	37	21	16	21	5	100
Free-Standing Low-Rise Apartments	18	44	18	12	6	98
Free-Standing High-Rise Apartments	5	0	10	58	26	99
High-Rise Projects	0	0	8	42	50	100
Low-Rise Projects	5	22	28	17	28	100
Garden-Type Apartments	36	21	21	7	14	99
Townhouse Apartments	31	12	25	12	18	98

*Totals not equal to 100 percent due to rounding.

of their negative responses to structure type. The
most frequently mentioned was that apartments do not
pay their full share of real estate taxes and, thus,
are a burden to the school district. A second frequently given reason was that apartments lower the
surrounding property values. A third fear was that
high-rise buildings would give the community the
appearance of a vertical slum, with southside Chicago
given as an example of what they do not want to happen
in their own communities. Lastly, and undoubtedly
not least important, is that they want to protect
their communities from a low-class invasion.

PUBLIC OFFICIALS' REACTIONS TO LOW
AND MODERATE INCOME GROUPS

Public officials were asked to project their
constituents' reaction to the prospect of the twelve
specified migrant groups moving into their community
under two assumptions: (a) that these households would
make up less than 10 percent, and (b) that they would
comprise more than 20 percent of the community's
population base.

The respondents were cautioned to ignore the
type of structures and to focus their attention on
the alternate household types. Again, if pressed as
to the type of structures, the interviewer replied--
similar to the type of structures now located in
your community. Although it cannot be guaranteed
that some respondents did not visualize an unattrac-
tive low-cost shelter, at least there is no reason
to believe that the majority answered the question
with that in mind.

Table 20 summarizes the officials' assumptions
of their constituents' reactions to each of the twelve
household types when these households constituted
less than 10 percent of their community. The greatly
and moderately accepting and moderately and greatly
unaccepting categories have been combined into one,
and percentages were computed for a single accepting
and unaccepting category. The public officials
hypothesized that, in general, black households and

TABLE 20

Public Officials' Projections of Their Constituents' Reactions to
to Low-/Moderate-Income Households Comprising
Less Than 10 Percent of Their Communities
(In Percent)

Income Groups	Accepting	Indifferent	Unaccepting	Total[a]
Low-Income[b] White--Elderly	61	17	22	100
Low-Income[b] Black--Elderly	11	17	72	100
Low-Income[b] White--Physically Handicapped	50	37	12	99
Low-Income[b] Black--Physically Handicapped	18	12	70	100
Low-Income[b] White--Husband	39	22	39	100
Low-Income[b] Black--Husband	17	17	66	100
Low-Income[b] White--No Husband	10	16	74	100
Low-Income[b] Black--No Husband	0	6	94	100
Moderate-Income[c] White--Husband	67	22	11	100
Moderate-Income[c] Black--Husband	42	10	47	99
Moderate-Income[c] White--No Husband	39	39	22	100
Moderate-Income[c] Black--No Husband	6	25	69	100

[a]Totals not equal to 100 percent due to rounding.
[b]Low income is under $5,000.
[c]Moderate income is $5,000-$10,000.

low-income households without a male head would be
the least acceptable. Thus, the least preferred
household type is the low-income black family without
husband. The second least preferred would be the
low-income white family without husband. The low-
and moderate-income black household with husband is
more acceptable, according to the respondents, than
either the black elderly or physically handicapped
households. The three most acceptable household
types are the moderate-income white family with husband, the white elderly, and the white physically
handicapped.

     Table 21 shows the reactions of the public offi-
cials under the assumption that the low- and moderate-
income households would constitute at least 20 percent
of the population base. Many public officials
expressed concern and, though apologetic, felt the
people they represented would not tolerate such high
levels of low-/moderate-income households moving
into their communities. All household types are
found to be less acceptable than those in Table 20,
which utilized the smaller percentage assumption.
In addition to this stronger objection to all household types, there are, also, some differences in
terms of the rank order of acceptability. For example,
the moderate-income black household with husband is
found to be as acceptable as moderate-income white
family with husband. The low-income white elderly
are now more acceptable than any other category.
Black families without husbands are viewed as completely unacceptable.

     Table 22 ranks the factors or reasons given by
the public officials for their constituents' opposition to the proposed entry of low-/moderate-income
groups. The anticipated drop in property values,
and race tie for the number one position. The racial
factor is particularly significant because it was
not directly on the questionnaire form but instead
was a "write-in." We do not know if, in the minds
of the public officials, race is being used as a
substitute for all the other stated objections.

     A drop in the quality of schools is ranked number
two. Most of the public officials were very sensitive

TABLE 21

Public Officials' Projections of Their Constituents' Reactions to
Low-/Moderate-Income Households Comprising at Least 20 Percent of the Community
(In Percent)

Income Groups	Accepting	Indifferent	Unaccepting	Total
Low-Income[a] White--Elerely	33	7	60	100
Low-Income[a] Black--Elerely	7	7	86	100
Low-Income[a] White--Physically Handicapped	20	20	60	100
Low-Income[a] Black--Physically Handicapped	7	0	93	100
Low-Income[a] White--Husband	18	12	70	100
Low-Income[a] Black--Husband	14	0	86	100
Low-Income[a] White--No Husband	7	0	93	100
Low-Income[a] Black--No Husband	0	0	100	100
Moderate-Income[b] White--Husband	26	30	44	100
Moderate-Income[b] Black--Husband	26	20	54	100
Moderate-Income[b] White--No Husband	12	31	57	100
Moderate-Income[b] Black--No Husband	7	7	86	100

[a]Low income is under $5,000.
[b]Moderate income is $5,000-$10,000.

TABLE 22

Factors That Influence the Rejection of Low-/Moderate-Income Groups,
Ranked by Importance
(In Percent)

Factors	Total Sample Very Important	Total Sample Important	Total Sample Unimportant	Total
Property Values Would Drop	50	35	15	100
Race*	50	--	--	50
Drop in Quality of Schools	47	37	16	100
Decrease in Law and Order	28	56	16	100
Property Taxes Would Increase Due to Need for Increased Services	28	28	43	99
Drop in Social Status	25	55	20	100
Housing Maintenance Would Decrease	25	50	25	100
People Would Not Fit In	16	72	11	99
Community Less Stable	11	67	22	100
Federal Government Interference*	11	--	--	11
Shift in Political Structure*	6	--	--	6
Change in Character of Community Shopping	0	21	79	100

*Race, federal government interference, and shift in the political structure were all write-ins and not on the questionnaire form. Therefore, we can assume all three would be very important to those specifying them and that their importance would have been greater had they been included directly on the questionnaire.

to this issue and, perhaps, credited it with more
importance than the suburbanites they represent. This
may be due to the fact that not all households have
children in the school system and that those without
children are, thus, less actively concerned. The
threat of a drop in property values and in the quality
of schools can be viewed as a direct threat to the
capital accumulation of the existing households.
The first would often affect the only savings pos-
sessed by the household, while the second threatens
the future ability of the household's children to
accumulate capital. The increase in property taxes
due to the need for increased services and a decrease
in law and order serve as the third most important
objection, while a drop in the community's social
status and a decrease in housing maintenance are a
close fourth. A drop in the community's social
status was far more important to those respondents
representing area 3--the higher status suburban com-
munity--than to those public officials affiliated
with less prestigious suburbs.

     Table 23 lists the responses of the public offi-
cials to the question of whether they personally, in
their present public roles, actively "encourage,"
"discourage," or "take no position" on such issues
as zoning and planning guidelines that would promote
the development of housing partially financed by a
variety of programs.

     Most indicated that they would actively discour-
age standard public housing projects coming into
their communities. Scattered public housing and
turnkey public housing programs appeared to be far
more acceptable alternatives. Several specified that
they would only encourage public housing programs
for their community's elderly, while others indicated
a reluctance to support any public housing that would
encourage the entry of lower-income households.
Table 23 suggests that Section 235 programs for
single-family residences would receive more encouragement than the Section 236 programs, which provide
multifamily residences for moderate-income households.
Seventy-two percent of the public official sample
said they would be supportive of Federal Housing

TABLE 23

Position of Public Officials on Alternately Financed Housing Programs
(In Percent)

Type of Financed Housing Programs	Encourage	Discourage	Take No Position	Total
Standard Public Housing Projects	17	72	11	100
Scattered Public Housing	61	28	11	100
Turnkey Public Housing	61	17	22	100
FHA Housing	72	11	17	100
VA Housing	67	11	22	100
Conventional	67	11	22	100
235 Single-Family Residences	61	22	11	100
236 Multifamily Residences	55	28	17	100

Administration (FHA) financed housing programs within
their area, while only 67 percent stated they would
encourage either Veterans Administration (VA) or conventional housing programs.

Each respondent was asked to identify those
groups, both formal and informal, which influenced
their thinking concerning the provision of low- and
moderate-income housing opportunities in the region.
This question elicited such a diversity of answers
that it is difficult to make any generalizations.
However, those officials representing area 3 felt
that most of the official and unofficial groups in
their jurisdiction would oppose the entry of low-
and moderate-income families.

In general, most of the public officials felt
that they would get adverse reactions from existing
senior citizens groups, who would oppose the possible
raising of their property taxes, as well as from
realtors and some developers. Church groups, some
citizen groups, the MVRPC, and the DMHA were seen as
positive pressure groups to promote the provision of
low- and moderate-income housing.

A serendipic effect of the public official survey was to provide the respondents an opportunity to
take time out from their busy lives to talk and think
about this very serious problem: How does a region
provide increased housing opportunities to its low-
and moderate-income households? Several began, in
the process of the interview, to reevaluate their
own position on these issues and to concern themselves with the problem of promoting positive social
change. These respondents not only gave their best
efforts to answering the questions summarized in
this chapter, but also formulated some challenging
questions of their own.

6

POSSIBLE IMPACTS
OF LOW AND MODERATE
INCOME HOUSING
ON THE NEIGHBORHOOD
ENVIRONMENT

"It is certainly better, however, to face
up to the situation than to incur further
alienation and frustration by promising to
correct the problem by means that are
bound to fail"[1]

The majority of the middle- and upper-income
residents of the suburbs that surround Dayton fear
that the entry of low- and moderate-income households
into their neighborhoods will harm important features
of their living environment. Specifically, they fear
that--

1. Property will be less well maintained.

2. Property values will drop.

3. Service levels will drop.

4. Property taxes will increase.

5. School quality will drop.

6. Social organization will deteriorate.

7. Social status will decline.

8. Social stability will decrease.

93

PROPERTY VALUES

Are the suburbanites' fears of a decline in
property values justified or unjustified? There is
evidence to suggest that, under some circumstances,
the movement of low- and moderate-income households
into an area has resulted in the feared consequences,
but, in other instances, this has not been so. The
actual results will vary with a number of factors,
many of which can be controlled if we understand
them and are willing to put forth the efforts and
resources required to control them. Thus, each
situation warrants a careful analysis of the underlying
forces affecting the neighborhood feature that is of
concern. To make this possible, the analyst must
know what underlying forces to look for and must not
confuse the issue with easy generalizations.

Perhaps, one of the best examples of confusion
is that surrounding the question of property values.
It has been vigorously argued that black entry into
a neighborhood either does or does not increase
property values. Before 1960, many real estate texts
and appraisal manuals indicated that the inclusion
of black residents in a neighborhood worked to
depress property values. This is not true; neither
should one believe the liberal propagandist who
asserts that black entry into a neighborhood always
makes prices rise.

In 1960, Luigi Laurenti considered the empirical
evidence gathered in seven cities where price movement
in neighborhoods that were receiving black residents
was compared with that in areas that had remained
all white. He reported that

> no single or uniform pattern of non-white
> influence on property prices could be de-
> tected. Rather, what happens to prices
> when non-whites enter a neighborhood seems
> to depend on a variety of circumstances
> which, in balance, may influence prices
> upward or downward or leave them unaf-
> fected.[2]

His conclusions confirmed prior statements by such
housing experts as Charles Abrams. Whether or not
prices will drop with the advent of a new group into
the neighborhood--in this case blacks--will depend
on the relative demands of the new and old residents
and on the relative supply of dwelling units open to
each.

If the effective demand for housing in the neighborhood on the part of blacks is more intense than
that of any other group, then, they will tend to drive
prices higher than would have been the case had the
barriers to black entry remained. Examples of this
can be found in older neighborhoods that excluded
blacks until vacancies encouraged someone to rent or
sell to them. Frequently, when the pent-up demand
of blacks was permitted to operate in the neighborhood, then the number of vacancies began to drop and
prices rose. This was the case for the West Philadelphia area reported on by Chester Rapkin and
William G. Grigsby.[3]

Conversely, it is possible for supply to eventually begin to climb faster than demand if the affluent
older group takes its dollar-bidding power away from
an existing neighborhood faster than the new group
can put up money. If this happens, prices will drop.
Rapkin and Grigsby reported on such a situation in
West Mount Airy, Philadelphia, in the same book in
which they had described the West Philadelphia
experience of black entry bringing with it the reverse
price effect.[4]

Thus, the placement of lower-income housing in
Dayton's suburban middle-income neighborhoods need
not cause the price of existing houses to drop. But
this could happen. It will happen if the present
residents start to leave and no other buyers or
renters with equal purchasing power seek to buy or
rent in their place. It will not happen if the same
class of people that is now in the neighborhood
continues to seek homes there. Of course, It can
also be guaranteed not to happen if the public treasury agrees to step in as a buyer should market prices
drop.

PROPERTY MAINTENANCE

    Maintenance involves spending in order to retard
or offset the tendencies toward deterioration. These
expenditures will be made if the property owner has
the incentive and the money required. If the property
is renter occupied, the landlord's incentive will
depend heavily on the economic pressure for maintenance
that his tenants are able to generate. One of the
tragedies of the 1950's and 1960's was that urban
renewal and highway programs cut the supply of older
lower-priced housing available, thereby forcing those
who would otherwise have been able to bargain for
more maintenance to accept less maintenance in the
only housing they could rent.[5] If renters are not
given a choice of other housing at similar prices,
there will be a tendency for the maintenance of
existing structures to slip. Conversely, if competitive supply conditions exist, rental housing will
tend to be well maintained, if the rents are high
enough to make such maintenance profitable.

    Of course, tenants can also create the need for
excessive maintenance by causing damage. Generally,
damage deposits and the threat of eviction are landlord weapons against such tenant behavior. However,
the owner of subsidized rental property may have
trouble using these weapons, in which case property
deterioration may increase. Certainly, this has
often been the case with public housing, though the
Dayton Metropolitan Housing Authority seems to be
doing an unusually good job of obtaining tenant cooperation. Nevertheless, there is always the problem
of providing incentives to encourage public housing
tenants to reduce the maintenance and repair costs
within their control.

    Stanley Lebergott has urged that every tenant
who generates below-average repair and maintenance
costs for his apartment unit receive a money payment
equal to that savings.[6] The Hawaii Housing Authority
is already successfully implementing a plan that goes
Lebergott one better. Unfortunately, the Hawaii
program is applicable only to that state's housing

projects in which income limits and rents are higher
than those applicable to federally subsidized low-
rent projects. Since 1964, families participating
in a plan set up by the state of Hawaii pay one-fifth
of their net family income to the housing authority.
The difference between the amount paid and the unit
operating cost is credited to the family's reserve
account, to be withdrawn as down payment on the purchase of a home. Jitsuri Yoshida, the Supervising
Public Housing Manager, indicated that, since the
passage of the plan in 1964 and September 30, 1970,
56 families have been assisted in becoming homeowners,
while 107 families were participating, with reserve
credits ranging from 2,000 to 6,000.

     There are many examples to show that lower-income
families will maintain property if they have the
resources and the incentive to do so. A recent
experiment in subsidizing and counseling low- and
moderate-income households so that they could become
homeowners reported their efforts to be successful,
but pointed to the need for child care facilities
to enable mothers to work and supplement the family
income--thereby enabling the family to meet the
financial responsibilities of home ownership.[7] Conversely, the slums provide proof of the drop in
maintenance that follows the occupancy by those who
have neither the personal resources to pay for expensive maintenance nor the market bargaining power to
force their landlords to do so. Thus, the direct
impact that the new residents make on maintenance
will depend greatly on the makeup of the programs
that enable them to move to the suburbs and the
selective process that determines the type of households that move into the new housing.

     However, the direct effect of the new resident
may not be as important as the results occasioned
by the local reaction to his arrival. If the new
residents alter the ability of the neighborhood to
attract the hold home buyers and renters of the class
that originally inhabited the neighborhood, then,
the overall level of maintenance will tend to drop.
Such a result follows because a drop in the income
level of the neighborhood residents would mean that,

all other things being equal, the new owners of
property would have less to spend on maintenance and
repair. In the long run, the impact of the new households on the neighborhood maintenance levels will
depend, at least to some degree, on whether or not
they cause the type of households presently in the
neighborhood to change their minds about the benefits
to be desired from living there.

One of the physical housing elements that our
survey indicated was influential in altering or
preserving current levels of desirability was the
compatibility and maintenance patterns of the new
units with the old. There are two aspects to this
element. One is the design of the new housing itself:
If not compatible with existing neighborhood standards,
it will alter the desirability of the neighborhood
in the eyes of present and potential future inhabitants
of the class now living there. Perhaps, the best
example of the worst kind of situation that could
develop would be construction of public housing units
that could not conform to neighborhood standards
because they had to conform to federal cost criteria.

For many years, housing experts have criticized
the design of public housing projects. Thirteen
years ago, Catherine Bauer Wurster, one of the early
advocates of public housing wrote that

> visually they may be no more monotonous
> than a typical suburban tract, but their
> density makes them seem more institutional,
> like veterans' hospitals or old-fashioned
> orphan asylums. The fact that they are
> usually designed as islands--'community
> units' turning their backs to the sur-
> rounding neighborhoods which look entirely
> different--only adds to their institutional
> quality.[8]

Wurster's conclusions were seconded by the renowned
housing expert William L. C. Wheaton, who suggested
that public housing should be designed and built
using the "best standards of the future, not the

worst standards of the past." Wheaton criticized
rigid federal design specifications and called for
a more flexible set of federal regulations.[9]

    To some degree, these criticisms and suggestions
have been heeded by the U.S. Department of Housing and
and Urban Development (HUD). Design controls are
more flexible now than they have been. But HUD will
have to be extremely flexible and willing to spend
if public housing units are to be accepted as blending
in with the buildings now prized by those living in
the suburbs. The San Francisco Housing Authority is
currently involved in an argument over design controls
and costs, in which local commission members are
charging that HUD is making it difficult for them to
provide 200 large-family housing units for thirty
scattered sites with the amenity features that they
consider desirable.[10]

    The question of providing public housing that
fits in with existing suburban housing illustrates
the problems that will have to be solved by any
subsidy program that puts low- and moderate-income
units into an existing middle-income suburban neighborhood. If the new units meet existing neighborhood
standards, then there is no reason that their physical
presence will alter the short- or long-run maintenance
standards by working to change the ability of the
neighborhood to attract and hold those who can and
will pay to preserve present levels of maintenance.
If the units clash with neighborhood standards, they
may engender instability. This could eventually
reduce the amount of money that the average residents
are willing and able to spend on maintenance by working
to change the socioeconomic makeup of the average
residents. Conversely, if the new units add to the
aesthetic appeal of the neighborhood, the long-run
effect may be to attract residents who will increase
the neighborhood's average maintenance level.

    While it is apparent that the long-run level
of neighborhood maintenance will be determined by
the host of primarily social factors that shape its
appeal to different groups, one other physical factor
is worth mentioning in the light of the information

provided by the suburban survey. Certain physical
elements of the housing environment have symbolic
values to some suburban residents. These symbolic
values are not shared by all households--including
some of the low- and moderate-income households that
need new dwelling units. For example, as pointed
out in Chapter 3, lawns have visual symbolic values
to the residents of many neighborhoods, particularly
in area 3--they are something to see, not to use.
If low- or moderate-income families who felt that
lawns were to be used for play, to sit upon, or to
display a prized couch were to move into the same
neighborhood, the older residents and those of their
class would perceive the neighborhood as having
become less desirable and, therefore, less worthy of
their own expenditure on maintenance.

PROPERTY TAXES AND GENERAL SERVICE LEVELS

Table 24 shows the direct expenditures for all
purposes of local government in Ohio during fiscal
year 1967/68. While expenditures in the five-county
Miami Valley region may not exactly fit this statewide pattern, the deviations will probably not be
dramatic. The majority of local funds are spent on
education, health and welfare, and public safety.
Although the needs of differing types of low- and
moderate-income households vary, many of these
households will require at least the average amount
of services that are currently provided and paid for
by the local community.

Since the property tax is still the backbone
of the local revenue system, and since the property
taxes generated by the typical low- and moderate-
income households may be less than average, there
is of course the possibility that the residents will
cause taxes to rise or service levels to drop. This
is particularly likely to be the case for low income
households. Dick Netzer of New York University has
studied the financial structures of several American
cities, including New York. He has pointed out that
most state and local taxes are regressive in their
incidence; that is, the taxes take out a smaller

TABLE 24

Direct Expenditures by Ohio Local
Government, 1967/68

Functional Area	Millions of Dollars	Percent
Education	$1,427.6	48
Highways	268.5	9
Public Welfare	128.0	4
Health and Hospitals	151.8	5
Police Protection	129.5	4
Fire Protection	78.0	3
Sewage	108.3	4
Sanitation Other than Sewage	49.9	2
Parks and Recreation	50.7	2
Finances Administration	34.7	1
General Control	78.9	3
Interest on Debt	108.4	4
Other	326.7	11
	$2,941.0	100

Source: U.S. Department of Commerce, Bureau of the Census, Governmental Finances in 1967-68 (Series GF 68, No. 5) (Washington, D.C.: U.S. Government Printing Office, September, 1969).

percentage of the income of the rich than middle-
income families. But he also reports that "it is
quite clear that on the average, state-local public
expenditure benefits to the poor far exceed the tax
burdens."[11]

There is certainly nothing surprising about the
possibility that suburban property taxes may rise or
service levels drop if more of the less affluent are
housed in the suburbs. The financial plights of many
large central cities have been well publicized as
being partly attributable to the high proportion of
the region's poor that they have kept within their
jurisdiction. The fact that they have tended to lose
a proportion of their businesses and industries to
the suburbs also contributes to the financial problem
of the center cities, as does the universal increase
in the demand for publicly provided services.

However, the role that the badly housed play
in financially burdening the city need not be reenacted
if some of them become well housed in the suburbs.
One of the reasons that the low- and moderate-income
groups who live in the central cities contribute
relatively little in taxes is that they live in old,
low-quality dwellings of relatively low market value.
Such units do not carry high property tax assessments.
However, this will not be the kind of housing provided
for the low- and moderate-income households that
are allowed to leave the central city and live in the
suburbs. Instead, the programs that enable them
to make this move will provide new, relatively high-
quality dwellings, with a market value fairly close
to the average value of the homes of the present
suburban property taxpayers.

Thus, the proposed low- and moderate-income
housing could contribute significantly to the tax
base of the suburbs. But will it?

The answer depends on the nature of the subsidy
program that permits the new dwelling units to be
built and occupied by households that, at least initially, cannot afford them. In the cities, most of
the small number of higher-quality units that have
been provided were paid by federal aid channeled

through the local public housing authority. The
Dayton Metropolitan Housing Authority, like any other
public housing authority, must live by the rules set
out by the money-granting federal government. Those
rules make the public housing units largely exempt
from the property tax; the in lieu payments that the
housing authority is allowed to make represent only
a small fraction of the property tax payments that
would derive from a privately owned unit of similar
value. Such exemptions are, in fact, a subsidy that
the local jurisdiction gives to occupants of the
publicly subsidized dwelling.

This tax deficiency of older public housing
programs is not present in the newer public housing
leasing programs. Under this program the owner
who leases his property to the local public housing
authority does pay property taxes.

It is interesting to note that the federal
government's right to claim such immunity from local
taxation was established in 1819 by the U.S. Supreme
Court in the case of McCulloch vs. Maryland. In
this case, Chief Justice John Marshall, made the
famous statement: "The power to tax involves the
power to destroy." This is still true, but the
jurisdictions have reversed roles since the 1819
case, and the "tax" that is being imposed on the
local jurisdiction is the subsidization of lower-
income households living in federally financed public
housing. The imposition of such a subsidy is sometimes not noted because it comes in the form of a
property tax exemption, in return for which the
local public housing agency gets the money it requires
to build housing for those who need it and cannot
afford to pay for it. But the exemption of property
from local taxes is an indirect subsidy and one that
the suburbs will resist paying.

Of course, no such subsidy will be wrung from
the suburbs if the new housing is built with the aid
of programs such as 235 or 236, which calls for the
full payment of property taxes. Neither would it
be imposed if the authorized in lieu payments were
set to equal the fair market value of structures
equivalent to the ones being built, or if the

government paid an amount equal to the costs of
providing the public services provided to the lower-
and middle-income residents. The amount of such
costs will vary with the composition of the low- and
moderate-income households that come to the suburbs.

The net direct fiscal effect of the new residents
will be affected by the makeup of their households,
the type of housing that is provided for them, and
the degree to which this housing is exempt from
local property taxes. Work in other areas suggests
that one should not too quickly prejudge the results
that will follow from a given "set" of these three
factors. For example, there is a fairly widespread
belief that single-family units are always more
fiscally rewarding than apartments. But a study by
the Prince George's County Economic Development
Committee suggests, at least in that county, that

> the average one- and two-family dwelling
> unit does not pay the direct cost to the
> county to educate one child or even to
> educate the .943 pupils per average unit
> in school for 1963-64--the much maligned
> apartment units pay their way, by an ample
> margin, for all services including the
> education of the .242 pupils per apartment
> unit in school for 1963-64.[12]

The net fiscal effects will also be influenced
by the degree to which the new residents cause
expansion in the capital and operating costs of the
services already being provided--that is, the degree
to which they cause marginal public costs to rise.
To take an extreme example: If the new households
can be serviced by the existing public work force
without any addition in hours worked and can be
handled by the physical capacity of the existing
capital facilities, then they would not cause the
tax rate to go up or service levels to decline, even
if the housing they lived in paid no property taxes.
The MVRPC was well aware of this effect when it
prepared the distribution plan that provided guidelines
allocating the 14,125 low- and moderate-income
dwelling units, which the five-county region needs,
to its fifty-three "planning units" or subareas.

The housing plan for the Miami Valley region minimizes the possibility that the provided new low- and moderate-income housing will burden the community, even if the units are provided by public housing. It does this by considering carefully the impact of housing on the critical service area of schooling. Distribution considered the existing position of the school system--the higher the assessed valuation per pupil, the greater the number of dwelling units assigned, and the more pupils "in excess of normal capacity, the fewer the units assigned."[13] If the implementation of this plan continues to consider this factor (and it is believed by the authors that it will) and if maximum use is made of programs that will pay property taxes, then the danger of a direct financial burden will be minimized.

The indirect and the long-run financial effects of the program will depend on what the new households and the existing residents do after the new units are occupied. If the new households whose housing will be improved due to the programs also gradually improve their economic lot, then the community gains will also expand through time. The skills and work that the residents bring to the community may well strengthen the economic base of the suburban area if these skills and work strength are employed.

Finally, the long-run indirect impact of the new households on taxes and service levels will depend on the reactions of the existing residents. Once again, the question of stability is raised. If the older households accept the new and do not flee from them, both can benefit. If the more affluent leave, or no longer are attracted into, the area in as great numbers, then the effect will be negative.

SCHOOL QUALITY

Since the costs of education make up a very large part of every community's budget, the factors discussed above are relevant to the subject of school quality. In fact, if money were the only determinant of school quality instead of merely an important one, the previous section would have been labeled "Property

Taxes, General Service Levels, and the Quality of
Education." It would then have been pointed out
that everything that could have been said about the
impact of the housing programs on the fiscal health
of suburban communities also applies to the schools.
The wisdom of estimating the number of children
included among the new residents to be admitted to
the suburbs, would have been emphasized, to make sure
that the programs that help them enter permit the
amount of money they contribute to the local public
treasury to equal the local school district's average
cost of schooling that many added pupils.

Such a dollar-oriented view of the impact of
the new households on the quality of education
should not be ignored. Teachers and those who maintain
and administer schools do have to be paid, as do the
contractors that build new schools. If all other
things are equal, the more money there is to pay
these contributors to our educational system, the
better the system will be. But all other things
are not equal. The quality of the school system
depends also upon many noneconomic factors. The way
the school is run and what it is teaching or seems
to be trying to teach the young can also be sources
of conflict only partly related to differences in
the financial results brought about by alternate
policies.

The members of any particular class tend to
have a fairly uniform idea of what they want from the
school system. In the Charles F. Kettering Foundation-
sponsored educational supplement of the Saturday
Review, Peter Schrag summarized what the more affluent
middle class who moved to the suburbs after World
War II wanted from their schools: "For the successful
in the suburbs the schools became contractual partners in a bargain that trades economic support
(higher taxes, teacher salaries, bond issues) for
academic credentials and some guarantee of advancement
in the form of college admission."[14]

However, as Herbert Gans pointed out in his
classic study of Levittown, N. J.: "The working
class who inhabit some suburban communities have a
different view of what the school system should

provide."[15] The working-class parent is generally
supportive of an education system that concentrates
on operating economically and instilling the vitures
of early self-sufficiency. They feel that the job
of the school is to produce economically self-sup-
porting youngsters who do not need four more years
of college plus graduate school before they can earn
a living. The working-class parent sometimes even
fears those options that promote upward mobility,
since this mobility is apt to draw their children
away from them both psycholocigally and physically.
They rarely see the need for "extras," such as music
lessons, drama, ballroom dancing, and other "social
frills."

Thus, there is often conflict, even between the
various groups that now inhabit the suburbs. Usually,
each community receives the type of educational
system its majority supports. But if the minority
is either sufficiently large or vocal, this generally
occurs only after a long, bitter struggle.*

It is interesting to identify the reactions of
the minority who do not get the type of school system
they desire or who are thwarted in some other significant area of their lives. If the minority is
affluent, its members generally elect to move to a
more compatible community. The less affluent are
often forced to remain and conform to the majority's
wishes. Thus, paradoxically, too great a heterogeneity
within a community tends toward homogeneity through
a voluntary exodus or enforced conformity of its
members.

The schools of the various suburban areas are
the product of the majority groups that inhabit the

------

*The Levittowners describes one such battle for
control of the school system between the working-
class Catholic parents and the middle class Protestant
families. The working-class parents, being in the
majority, won the battle for control of the school
board.

areas today. There is evidence to suggest that
these schools may be disruptively impacted if significant numbers of former central city pupils are assigned to them without any special attention being
paid to the problems that such assignments might bring.
The most recent and well-documented evidence is
found in a special research report of a study conducted by the Syracuse University Research Corporation
of disruption in urban public secondary schools.[16]
However, the need for special planning to precede
the movement of significant numbers of central city
students to the suburbs was pointed out to us in
an interview with one of the local school officials
before the nationwide Syracuse study was released.

The Syracuse study confirmed the fact that a
large proportion of our urban public schools have
suffered disruption: 85 percent of the urban schools
responding to their survey had experienced some
type of disruption in the past three years. The
most common were student boycotts, walkouts, or
strikes; teacher boycotts, walkouts, or strikes;
arson; property damage other than arson; rioting;
student-teacher physical confrontation; picketing
or parading; presence on campus of unruly, unauthor-
rized nonschool persons; and abnormal unruliness.
Racial issues were a factor in a significant proportion
of these disruptions.

Studies like the Syracuse study are extremely
valuable because they face and reveal the existence
of a problem; it is unfortunate that few such
scholarly reports on the problem exist. They point
out that we have several elements in our society
that work to encourage such disruptions, particularly
on the part of those who have long been poor and
discriminated against. They also point out that
the ghetto environment that many of the young people
must return to each night makes it particularly
difficult for them to "perform more or less like
their middle class compatriots."[17] The program
that will provide suburban housing opportunities
will take the pupils out of such environments and,
if they are sufficiently sensitive and comprehensive,
could help them adjust to a new environment that they
live in and are not bused to.

The Syracuse study also indicates that there
was a series of complex "in-school causes" for the
disruptions. These causes included some "cross-
cultural clashes" due partly to the difficulty that
teachers and staff have in making needed adjustments
to changing social mix. The schools of the Miami
Valley region can prepare themselves for the new
students so as to make the adjustments required for
educational quality.

The knowledge of what could go wrong can make
possible the development and implementation of
programs that bring the new households into the
educational system of the suburbs without disruption.
This is especially true of the MVRPC plan, which
calls for the entrance of a relatively small number
of low- and moderate-income households into the
suburbs. Some additional suggestions on this subject
are presented in Chapter 9. Once again, neighborhood
stability will be a significant factor in achieving
the improvement of, or at least the maintenance of,
educational quality. If the more affluent begin to
leave the neighborhoods or the schools, it will be
increasingly difficult to maintain the economic
or social viability of the educational system.

SOCIAL ORGANIZATION

Urban experiences have been cited to demonstrate
the apparent and possible positive and negative
effects of programs that permit the construction
of needed housing for low- and moderate-income
households in the suburbs. The critical factors
that will interrelate to determine the effects have
also been pointed out, and there has been an attempt
to suggest how the suburbs can benefit from the
urban experience of recent decades.

The importance of not duplicating the pattern
of social organization that has typified the recent
urban experience of the low- and, to a much lesser
extent, moderate-income households, is too obvious
to warrant lengthy discussion. In fact, one of the
basic goals of the Miami Valley Regional Housing
Plan is "to create and/or maintain sound, viable

neighborhoods in the process of housing those people."[18]
Today's urban ghettoes are usually too shabby, as
well as functionally obsolete. Street patterns and
public service facilities are frequently obsolete
or inefficient. Lot layouts are often inappropriate
for both public and private facilities, while many
existing housing structures are overcrowded or in
less than standard condition. The social environment
may also be undesirable. Households with differing
capacities, abilities, motivations, and life styles
are often forced to live together because they are
poor or black. Thus, the prostitute and the thief
are not separated from the family trying to advance
economically and socially through legitimate channels.
The latter must be given the opportunity of escaping
from the physical and cultural poverty of his surroundings.

There is little to suggest that new and healthy
patterns of social organization would result from
merely providing new housing for those who are now
unemployed, alienated, and socially disorganized.[19]
A greater number of low-income inhabitants of the
present central city slums are more likely to be
disoriented and prone to socially and self-destructive
acts than an average sampling of the American population. Therefore, a random selection of the central
city low-income population would tend to be socially
disorganized. But there is no reason why those who
accept the opportunities presented by the expansion
of subsidized low- and moderate-income housing
programs in the suburbs should be randomly selected.
In fact, our survey suggests that a self-selection
of such opportunities by low-income households
would be far from random.

The social organization that will result as
suburban housing opportunities are grasped will
depend upon the makeup of the households that are
involved and the social patterns that they are
allowed to create. One bad example already exists
in the Miami Valley region. One subsidized rental
housing project in a suburban community was shown
to us where students who "paid the full rent" were
allowed to move into some of the apartments of a

project that also housed low-income families. The
families were given little help in adjusting to this
new environment and no choice as to their neighbors
in the project. It was told to us that the students
not only "generally raised hell" but also used and
sold drugs. When asked why the students were allowed
to move in, the reply was: "The federal regulations
require that a proportion of nonsubsidized tenants
be included in all such projects."

The project (just referred to) was built in a
predominantly rural portion of the region before
the MVRPC plan was completed. It demonstrates the
need for careful implementation of programs that
provide suburban housing opportunities. There has
been little opportunity for such experiences to be
gained. But the experience gained by leaders in
the innovational development of low- and moderate-
income housing in suburbia, such as Dorothy Duke,
suggests that strong and beneficial patterns of
social organization can be developed.* It appears
likely that successful efforts will concentrate on
helping those who have the capability and incentive
to adopt beneficial patterns of social organization
and to do so in a decent housing environment, instead
of concentrating on providing therapy to those who
do not want to do so. It also appears more than

----

*Dorothy Duke indicated that Turnkey III, a
new administrative housing program that facilitates
home ownership for the low income, has been successful in Gulfport and Fernshaw County, Mississipi. The
program requires the recipients to pay out only 20
percent of their income for new housing and has
maintenance incentives built into the plan that enable
the household to transfer maintenance savings into
downpayment credits. Duke feels strongly that it
is not sufficient to provide a structure, but that
a supportive services program is necessary for
prospective tenants. Her main concern has been to
provide more housing opportunity for low- income
black households and has been far less concerned
with integration and other social goals.

likely that the 14125 housing units that the MVRPC
has called for can be filled with such people.

SOCIAL STABILITY AND STATUS

Many of the possibilities for beneficial results
that have been discussed above depend to some degree
on the maintenance of social stability following
the announcement, construction, and habitation of
the new housing. It is important that the level
of social heterogeneity introduced into the neighborhood or community be maintained. As indicated, this
can only happen if the neighborhood or community
continues to be attractive to the type of people
that lived in it before the housing programs were
inaugurated. Such social stability can be achieved,
but the experiences of those who have achieved it
suggest that this is not easy

The problems and opportunities for social
stability were explained to us by Morris Milgram
and his wife, Jean Gregg Milgram, the Executive
Director of National Neighbors, an organization of
interracial neighborhood associations. Milgram, a
builder and developer, who has worked for years at
building and operating mixed racial developments,
says stability can best be achieved if the rate of
in-movement is carefully controlled. He said that
there was no single "tip point" after which a mass
exodus took place, but that the flow of new residents
is constantly being observed by those who live in
the development or are considering moving in.

Because of racial bias, it is difficult to
maintain a new level of stability once a new racial
group has been introduced. But it does happen--and
with increasing frequency. However, a second element
is introduced by class heterogeneity. Furthermore,
there are some basic forces that work to preclude the
development of extremely heterogeneous neighborhoods.

The MVRPC was cognizant of the importance of
maintaining neighborhood stability, and, thus, their
plan concentrated on the goal of providing opportunity

for all the region's households rather than promoting
large-scale class integration on the neighborhood
level as a social goal per se. However, it is
important to point out the relationship between social
stability, status, and class heterogeneity, since
some of our national policy-makers hold conflicting
social goals implicitly, as well as explicitly.

The desire for exclusive residential enclaves
is directly related to the degree of class mobility
within a society. In societies with entrenched
caste systems, in which every person knows his/her
place, status is not determined or announced by
residential location.

In our society, upward mobility has been a
prerequisite to a move to an exclusive residential
location. Gans states: "People do not live in the
political units we call 'cities' or 'small towns',
often their social life is in areas even smaller
than a census tract. Many such areas in the city
are about as homogeneous in class as Levittown; and
slum and high-income areas, whether urban or suburban,
are even more so. Small towns are notoriously rigid
in their separation of rich and poor, and only appear
to be more heterogeneous because individual neighborhoods are so small. All these considerations effectively question the belief that, before the advent
of modern suburbs, Americans of all classes lived
together. Admittedly, statistics compiled for cities
and suburbs as a whole show that residential segregation by class and by race are on the increase,
but these trends also reflect the breakdown of rigid
class and caste systems, in which low-status people
'knew their place' and which made residential segregation unnecessary."[20]

Gan's penetrating study of Levittown, N. J.,
suggested that extreme heterogeneity encouraged
more conflict than integration. He concluded that
"while conflict can be desirable and even didactic,
this is only true if it can be resolved in some way.
People so different from each other in age or class
that they cannot agree on anything are not at liberty
to derive much enrichment from heterogeneity.[21]

Extreme heterogeneity is generally accompanied by vast differences in child-rearing practices, social customs, future versus present orientations to life, and a host of other values, attitudes and preferences that are often included in the term "life style."

One generalization appears to be true and must be considered as it relates to the goal of establishing heterogeneous neighborhoods. Each group holds its own life style to be the appropriate one, while viewing those that differ with varying degrees of mistrust and hostility.

What are some of these life-style differences? Bennett M. Berger in his study of auto workers in suburbia states that the "working class suburbs are not characterized by future orientation, aspirations for personal achievement, etc."[22] Their orientation is to life-influenced leisure-time activities, friendship cliques, child-rearing practices, and practically every other facet of life. For example, these working-class families seldom sought friends from place of work or the neighborhood; rather, the church and relatives were the primary sources for socializing. The working-class household seldom entertained. For example: "Wine with dinner is not conceived as a nice middle-class habit, wine with dinner is a 'Dago' habit--something that goes with spaghetti, ravioli, and lasagna."[23] Berger's study revealed that television was the main source of entertainment, with Westerns and sports shows being most preferred, since they were not identified with middle-class life styles.

In contrast to the middle-class mother who spends many of her hours reading and discussing child-rearing practices, Berger found that 43 percent of the working-class mothers read nothing at all on child rearing. Twenty-six percent said they did read books on this subject but disagreed with the conclusions. Most were proud to say: "I don't go by the book."

In neighborhoods with highly diverse life styles, child-rearing practices often become a major source

of conflict. For example, the working-class mother
tends to be strict with the very young child and
permissive with the adolescent. The upper middle-
class mother generally reverses such practices.
Should these women live near each other, conflict
is likely to arise at both child-rearing stages.
When their respective toddlers fight over a possession,
one mother will feel the child should be disciplined,
the other, that the child should not be remonstrated,
since he is just going through a natural stage in
development. During the teenage period, the upper
middle-class mother expects her child to study
seriously so that he can get into college; therefore,
she watches his time allocation closely. The working-
class mother permits her teenager a great deal more
freedom, since he (or she) will soon be on his own
and taking responsibility for his own actions.

While conflict may induce enforced conformity,
not all conformity can be so classified. Gans
specifies three types:

1. Wanted conformity where neighbors learn
    from each other to share ideas volun-
    tarily.

2. Tolerated conformity is where they
    adjust their own standards voluntarily
    to maintain friendly relations.

3. Unwanted conformity is a bow to pres-
    sure and the giving up of individual-
    ity.

According to Gans, the working class generally
experiences this kind of situation.[24]

If the first type of conformity is encouraged,
neighborhood stability will be preserved. If the
second type is forced, stability may not result
because many of the suburbanites have the economic
power to move--and may do so. Certainly, this is
true for the third type of conformity that Gans
cites.

Thus, the preservation of stability depends upon developing housing patterns that primarily require the first type of conformity, little of the second, and none of the third. The following chapter reports on the attempt by us to gain empirical insight into the factors that make such housing developments possible.

NOTES

1. Richard Muth, discussing the elimination of racial residential segregation in his article, "The Urban Economy and Public Problems," in Financing the Metropolis, ed. John P. Crecine (Beverly Hills, Calif.: Sage Publications, 1970), p. 456.

2. Luigi Laurenti, Property Values and Race: Studies in Seven Cities (Berkeley: University of California Press, 1960).

3. Chester Rapkin and William G. Grigsby, The Demand for Housing in Racially Mixed Areas (Berkeley and Los Angeles: University of California Press, 1960), pp. 98-102.

4. Ibid., pp. 125-38.

5. Claude Gruen, "Urban Renewal's Role in the Genesis of Tomorrow's Slums," Land Economics, XXXIX, No. 3 (August 6, 1963); also, Muth, op. cit., pp. 443-48.

6. Stanley Lebergott, "Slum Housing: A Proposal," The Journal of Political Economy, LXXVIII, No. 6 (November-December 1970), pp. 1362-66.

7. The San Francisco Development Fund, Summary Report on a Move to Home Ownership (December, 1970), p. 10.

8. Catherine Bauer, "The Dreary Deadlock of Public Housing," Architectural Forum (May, 1957), p. 141.

9. William L. C. Wheaton, Architectural Forum
(June, 1957), p. 141.

10. San Francisco Chronicle, February 12, 1971.

11. Dick Netzer, "Tax Structures and Their
Impact on the Poor," in Financing the Metropolis,
op. cit., p. 460.

12. Economic Development Committee of Prince
George's County, "A Study of Income and Expenditures
by Family Dwelling, Apartment and Business Units
and Individual School Children for the Fiscal Year
1963-64" (1963), Section V. Prince George's County,
Md.: October, 1963.

13. Miami Valley Regional Planning Commission,
A Housing Plan for the Miami Valley Region Suburbs
(1970), pp. 27-28.

14. Peter Schrag, "End of the Impossible Dream,"
Saturday Review (September 19, 1970), p. 92.

15. Herbert Gans, The Levittowners: Ways of
Life and Politics in a New Suburban Community (New
York: Vintage Books, 1969).

16. Stephen K. Bailey, Disruption in Urban
Public Secondary Schools (Washington, D.C.: National
Association of Secondary Schools Principals, November,
1970).

17. Ibid., p. 20.

18. Miami Valley Regional Planning Commission,
op. cit., p. 3.

19. See, for example, Daniel M. Wilners, The
Housing Environment and Family Life (Baltimore:
Johns/Hopkins Press, 1962).

20. Gans, op. cit., p. 165.

21. Ibid., p. 170.

22.   Bennett M. Berger, Working Class Suburb:
A Study of Auto Workers in Suburia (Berkeley and
Los Angeles: University of California Press, 1960),
p. 97.

23.   Ibid., p. 79.

24.   Gans, op. cit., p. 180.

7

**FACTORS
THAT MAKE
A STABLE MIXED
RESIDENTIAL
COMMUNITY**

"The most impressive thing to me about the entire
Hyde Park-Kenwood experience is that various
segments of the community found the will to
modify their initial positions to accept less
than they liked and to work together over a
long period of time to make the compromise a
reality."[1]

A NATIONWIDE SAMPLE OF MIXED RESIDENTIAL
NEIGHBORHOODS AND COMMUNITIES

Chapter 6 has indicated that the manner of arrival of low-and moderate-income households into the
suburbs, which affects critical aspects of the neighborhood environment, is closely linked to the question
of neighborhood social stability. To gain insight
into the causes or likelihood of stability, examples
of what is happening to areas that contain one or all
of the following kinds of mixing or integration were
sought:

1. Economic--households with widely diverging
incomes living in the same block, neighborhood, or
community

2. Sociocultural--households with greatly differing values and life styles (i.e., differing

119

household types) living in the same block, neighborhood, or community

    3.   Racial

    4.   Structural--single-family and multiunit
dwellings being mixed in the same block, neighborhood,
or community.

    Ninety-one questionnaires were sent out, asking
initially: "Do you know of any residential areas
that provide housing for low and moderate income
households that contain a wide range of economically,
socially or racially divergent residents and/or contain a variety of structural types?" (A copy of the
complete questionnaire is presented in Appendix H,
with a cover letter that accompanied it. Respondents
were asked to fill out the questionnaire or, if they
preferred, to call us collect at our San Francisco
office.)

    The questionnaire was open-ended but it did ask
for comment on whether the mixing had been a success
or failure--how stable they believed the present mix
to be and what they thought the future makeup of the
area would be. We also asked what impact the area
or project had had on the larger community.

    The list of individuals to be mailed question-
naires was initially compiled by the MVRPC staff and
by us. However, as the study progressed, additional
names were referred to us and added to the list.

    The final survey included regional and local
planners, redevelopment personnel, developers, pro-
fessors, housing commission members, and HUD officials. Forty-five percent of all those receiving
questionnaires responded by completing the form or
by telephoning us. Of all those who responded,
50 percent stated that they did know of at least one
development or neighborhood that was heterogeneous
in makeup and described the area in terms of its location, size, type of development or project, and the
type and degree of mixing.

TYPE OF RESPONSES RECEIVED

Perhaps, the first important finding of this
survey of knowledgeable housing experts is the fact
that 50 percent of the responses were negative, that
is, the respondent did not know of any area that was
significantly integrated in terms of race, economic,
or sociocultural mix. This is not surprising, but it
does tend to confirm the commonly held belief that
we are a nation of relatively homogeneous neighborhoods. Table 25 presents the geographical sample
distribution. The Northeast accounted for the largest
number of sample replies, or ten more than the Southeast, which contained the fewest. The West/Southwest
had the highest response rate; the Northeast the
lowest. The Midwest and Northeast made more positive
nominations, while the West and Southeast the fewest.

All but two of the nineteen nominated communities
were located in central cities, many being part of
urban redevelopment projects originating in the 1950's.
The two exceptions are the "new towns," or Columbia,
Maryland, and Reston, Virginia.

The accuracy of neither the descriptive nor
evaluative responses has been verified, though the
knowledge and thoughtfulness of many respondents
impressed us. A summary description of the nineteen
areas that were discussed by the respondents is presented in Appendix I. Two differing descriptions of
Mount Airy in Philadelphia were received, and both
have been presented in Appendix I; the respondents
may have been referring to different parts of Mount
Airy. Three descriptions of San Francisco's Diamond
Heights area were also received, but, since the
information received was similar, they are reported
as one.

It was interesting to note that one respondent
felt that the city of San Jose, California, should
be included as a project, since it contained neighborhoods that differed from each other in respect to
the demographic and socioeconomic makeup of residents.

TABLE 25

Geographical Distribution of Responses

Geographic Area	Positive Nominations		Negative Responses		No Response		Total of Mailed Questionnaires[a]	
	Number	Percent	Number	Percent	Number	Percent	Number	Percent
Northeast[b]	7	25	4	14	17	61	28	100
Southeast	2	11	6	33	10	55	18	99
Midwest[b]	8	38	1	5	12	57	21	99
West/Southwest[b]	4	17	9	37	11	46	24	100
Total	21		20		50		91	

[a]Totals do not equal 100 percent due to rounding.
[b]The geographic section contains at least one project or community that has been nominated by two or more individuals.

122

This nomination has been included, not only because
it was desired to report all replies that had been
received, but, also, because it indicated that even
a fast-growing city conforms to the typical citywide
patterns noted in Chapter 3. (The traditional role
of the city has been to sustain a wider range of homogeneous neighborhoods than is found in the suburbs.
This is because the oldest housing of most regions,
sought by the poor because they can afford it, is
usually found in the central city.)

The size of the nineteen nominated areas varied
considerably. Five communities were 1,000 acres or
less, while seven were from 2,000-7,500 acres. The
smallest nomination consisted of 125-175 acres; the
largest city of San Jose. In addition to San Jose,
there were six "no answers" to this question. An
analysis of the survey responses does not suggest
any direct relationship between the size of the community and the success of the project. Excluding the
two new town communities of Reston and Columbia, none
of the respondents nominated an exisitng suburban
community that was integrated by race, class, or
sociocultural mix.

THE NINETEEN NOMINATED AREAS GROUPED
BY TYPE OF ECONOMIC MIX

Table 26 categorizes the responses that were
obtained by grouping them first into six categories
that were based on the kind of economic mix that was
indicated.

Two project nominations, the Lower East Side in
New York and the Lynn Corporation development in
Indianapolis, fall into the first categorization,
which contains a range of "low- to moderate-" income
households. Although both were described as extremely
heterogeneous in the sociocultural, racial, and
structural mix, neither was evaluated in terms of the
project's success.

Five areas were depicted as containing "low- to
high-" income residents. These areas are the following:

1. Mount Airy Neighborhood--Philadelphia,
    Pennsylvania

2. South End Neighborhood--Boston, Massachusetts

3. Lincoln Park Community--Chicago, Illinois

4. Park Hill--Denver, Colorado

5. The city of San Jose, California.

This category includes two sets of responses for
Mount Airy, Philadelphia. As indicated above, the
discrepancies between the two descriptions of Mount
Airy may be due to the fact that the respondents
were depicting different geographic entities. However, this is only a hypothesis, since neither
answered the question dealing with the size of the
area. Mount Airy elicited two differing evaluations
of the success of the community. One stated unequivo-
cally that Mount Airy was a nationally known example
of a successfully integrated project. The second
gave a more qualified evaluation of the project's
success and commented that the families moving into
the large homes generally send their children to a
private school. This would suggest an area that
provides a good housing buy for the family desirous
of obtaining more housing space and quality than
could be purchased in an area that provides "good
schools" as part of a higher social status package.
Thus, for some, it may be more desirable and less
costly to send their children to private school than
to purchase an equivalent house in an area noted for
its good schools.

    All five of these areas were stated to be mixed
racially and socioculturally. Three were said to
provide a diverse housing mix, while the South End
neighborhood in Boston and Denver's Park Hill area
consisted primarily of single-family residences.
The Mount Airy area was described alternatively as
providing a mixture of multifamily units and as providing a combination of single- and multifamily
residences.

TABLE 26

Characteristics of the Positive Nominations
as Drawn from the National Survey

(a)

Low to Moderate Income (Under $10,000)
--two Responses

Sociocultural Mix:	2--Extremely heterogeneous in terms of age and life cycle status, occupational diversity, and ethnicity.
Racial Mix:	1--White, black, and Oriental (no percentage breakdown).
	1--Over 50 percent black.
Structural Mix:	1--Mixture of multifamily units. 1--Mixture of multi- and single-family units.
Number of Units:	1--Under 5,000.
	1--No answer.
Degree of Success in Terms of Stability and Organization:	2--No answer.

(b)

Low to High Income[a]--six Responses

Sociocultural Mix:	6--Extremely heterogeneous in terms of age and occupational status.
Racial Mix:	1--Mixed (no percentage breakdown).

(Continued)

TABLE 26 (Continued)

Characteristics of the Positive Nominations
as Drawn from the National Survey

(b)

Low to High Income[a]-- (Continued)

	1--Under 20 percent black. 3--20-50 percent black. 1--Over 50 percent black.
Structural Mix:	1--Single-family only. 1--Mixture of multifamily. 4--Mixture of multi- and single-family.
Number of Units:	1--5,000-10,000. 2--10,000-20,000. 1--Over 20,000. 2--No answer.
Degree of Success in Terms of Stability and Organization:	1--Families with children moving out due to increase in gang activity, with concomitant increase in childless population and single adults. 1--Professionals moving back into area. Community organizations have helped to stabilize neighborhood by working to maintain a single-family area and the quality of education. Class friction evident. 1--Mount Airy neighborhood-- Example of nationally known successfully integrated project.

TABLE 26 (Continued)

Characteristics of the Positive Nominations
as Drawn from the National Survey

(b)

Low to High Income[a]-- (Continued)

	1--Community organization active. Families moving into large homes send children to private schools. 2--No answer.

(c)

Moderate Income (Over $5,000 to Under $15,000)
--five Responses

Sociocultural Mix:	5--Not a great diversity. Most households are family units.
Racial Mix:	2--Under 20 percent black. 3--80-100 percent black.
Structural Mix:	1--Single-family only. 2--Similar multifamily units. 2--Mixture of multifamily units.
Number of Units:	2--Under 1,000. 2--5,000-10,000. 1--10,000-15,000.

(Continued)

TABLE 26 (Continued)

Characteristics of the Positive Nominations
as Drawn from the National Survey

───

(c)

Moderate Income (Over $5,000 to Under $15,000)
(Continued)

───

Degree of Success
  in Terms of Stability
  and Organization: 1--No housing mix, but racial
                                 mix stable at 11 percent.
                              1--No racial mix, but housing
                                 mix.
                              1--Racial mix (20 percent
                                 black), but no class mix.
                              2--No answer.

───

(d)

Moderate to High Income (Over $6,000)
--four Responses

───

Sociocultural Mix: 4--Not a great diversity in
                                 in terms of class.
                                 Mostly family households.

Racial Mix: 2--Under 20 percent black.
                              1--20-50 percent black.
                              1--No answer.

Structural Mix: 1--Multifamily only.
                              3--Mixture of single- and
                                 multifamily units.

Number of Units: 1--1,000-5,000.
                              2--5,000-10,000.
                              1--No answer

128

TABLE 26 (Continued)

Characteristics of the Positive Nominations
as Drawn from the National Survey

(d)

Moderate to High Income (Over $6,000)
(Continued)

Degree of Success in Terms of Stability and Organization:	3--Racial, but no class integration. 1--No answer.

(e)

Other Economic Mixes[b]--two Responses

Sociocultural Mix:	2--No answer.
Racial Mix:	1--50 percent black. 1--No answer.
Structural Mix:	2--Wide variety.
Number of Units:	2--1,000-5,000.
Degree of Success in Terms of Stability and Organization:	1--Not been in existence long enough to answer. 1--No answer.

(Continued)

TABLE 26 (Continued)

Characteristics of the Positive Nominations
as Drawn from the National Survey

(f)

Economic Mix-- No Answer-- one Response

Sociocultural Mix:	1--Heterogeneous in terms of occupational mix.
Racial Mix:	1--95 percent black.
Structural Mix:	1--Mixed single and multi-family units.
Number of Units:	1--Under 1,000.
Degree of Success in Terms of Stability and Organization:	1--Class but no racial integration.

---

aThis category includes the city of San Jose. It also includes the response data from two questionnaires that give disparate descriptions of the Mount Airy Neighborhood in Philadelphia. One respondent said Mount Airy contained 60 percent black, 15,000 housing units, and 26 percent of the households with incomes in excess of $10,000. The second said the area was 30-40 percent black, that it contained 5,000-10,000 units, and that 40 percent of all households earned in excess of $20,000. These discrepancies may be due to the fact that the description encompassed different geographical areas. Neither respondent identified the size of the area on the questionnaire form.

bCould not specify as to economic mix. One area was classified as diverse, and the other is currently in the process of being rented.

These five low- to high-income projects attracted
a variety of responses to the questions that sought
an evaluation of their success. A summary of the
responses includes two "no answers," one indication
of unstability and a resultant change in the household
makeup, one qualified success story, and a more
lengthy description of a designated successful project.

Neither San Jose nor the South End neighborhood
project answered the question that dealt with success.
The Lincoln Park community in Chicago was described
as an area in transition. The respondent indicated
that families with children were moving out because
of an increase in gang activity. However, he also
felt there appeared to be a concomitant increase of
single adults and childless households.

The Park Hill community in Denver, Colorado, was
stipulated a successful project. The respondent in
this instance was an "expert" in two respects. Pro-
fessionally, he had worked in the area as a member
of the planning community, in addition to being a
resident. He believes that attitudes related to
economic groups create more neighborhood friction
than those related to racial integration. He strongly
suggests the community organizations have had a positive impact upon the stability of the area--that they
have promoted a well-maintained single-family area
and have attempted to improve the school system. A
May 3, 1970, Denver Post newspaper article describing
the Park Hill community makes reference to some of
these organized efforts. A general description of
the area includes the following: "The houses are
imaginative and different, with a wide range of styles
that includes Spanish, English, and Colonial and
ranging in value from $10,000-85,000. Whether modest
or mansion, most are set in lawns that show much
loving care."[2] We know from our regional survey, as
well as the literature search, just how important the
maintenance of the exterior house and yard is to the
suburbanite neighbors. The community organizations
have also served to promote an increased enforcement
of housing codes and have attempted to keep commercial
activities from encroaching on the existing neighborhoods. The article goes on to detail that "much

attention is paid to the school system, trying to get more minority teachers, urging that minority history be taught, setting up a human relations commission."[3]

Perhaps, an integral part of this project's success, as well as the success of others, is the process of self-selection. Thus, " . . . people who move into Park Hill most often do so because of their belief in participating in an integrated society."[4] The article points out the paradoxical situation that "just as often they find they really aren't getting to know any of their neighbors."[5] However, the community organizations do appear successful in bringing together diverse groups in formalized get-togethers such as wine-tasting parties. Thus, it appears that friendship relationships continue to depend on more than physical proximity.

The third major category of areas presented in Table 26 includes five that are primarily inhabited by moderate-income family households. Three of the areas--Hempstead, River House Apartments, and Stone Keygate--are either primarily or entirely inhabited by black households. Uniondale and the Lafayette-Elmwood projects contain less than 20 percent minority group members. Two of the five projects provide a mixture of low- and high-rise apartments. Two provide homogeneous apartment structures, while one consists of only single-family detached houses.

Since the five areas are categorized by their relatively limited economic range, the successful mixing evaluations must be based on other criteria. Uniondale and Lafayette-Elmwood are considered to be examples of a stable racially integrated area. Eleven percent of the Uniondale households are minority group residents, while the Lafayette-Elmwood project consists of 19 percent black in its low-rise and 10 percent black in its high-rise apartments. The Hempstead project was said to be mixed solely in terms of its housing structures. None of the three was postulated to provide an example of class integration. No evaluations were given for the Stone Keygate and River House projects.

Additional background material on the Elmwood
Park area, which is now in the process of constructing
some low-income units to be located in Elmwood
was sent to us. The impact of these unfinished units
is, of course, unknown at this time. Initially, low-
income blacks were moved out of the area and their
housing cleared to create new housing for middle-
income white and black residents. Currently, the
middle-income parents send their children to all but
one of the public schools in the area. The exception
is an elementary school that serves an adjacent lower-
income population. A description of the area, furnished by the Mayor's Committee for Community Renewal,
states: "It is obvious that unless parents feel their
children will have a significant number of similarly
raised friends in attendance, they will not send their
children to school."[6]

Four projects are designated as communities
containing moderate- to high-income households. Each
was thought to provide little diversity as to sociocultural mix, and each was thought to consist primarily of family households. All four areas were
described as racially integrated and were believed
to contain a variety of structural units, with three
providing both single-family and apartment residences.
The four areas were the following:

1. Columbia, Maryland

2. Reston, Virginia

3. Diamond Heights--San Francisco, California

4. Hyde Park-Kenwood--Chicago, Illinois.

The report on Reston did not contain a discussion of
the success of the new town. The three respondents
who presented data on the San Franciso Diamond Heights
redevelopment project felt that it had successfully
mixed the moderate with the middle income. They
attributed a good measure of this success to the fact
that all of the moderate-income households had been
carefully screened. Despite this fact, one respondent
remarked that sales were slower directly across from

the moderate-income units than elsewhere in the project. The respondents also commented on the beneficial effect of designing fourplexes to look like two individual townhouses.

Respondents reporting on the Columbia and the Hyde Park-Kenwood areas stated that those were examples of successful racial, but not class, integration.

It was learned from a telephone conversation with one of Columbia's planners that Columbia contained no welfare or aid-to-dependent children families. The lower moderate-income households consisted of younger households of similar class status. He pointed out that the 235 and 236 households were generally young couples, secretaries, or divorcees. Reston also informed us that they currently had no low-income residents and that their moderate-income housing was generally sought by young families. However, they have plans to build ten public housing units at some future time. The River Acres project in Mt. Clemens, Michigan; has provided 20 scattered public housing units in its 450-unit development. Excluding the city of San Jose as not being directly comparable, the River Acres community is the only nominee currently providing public housing options.

Supplementary background material on the Hyde Park-Kenwood area, in the form of a well-documented case history of the community, was provided by an illustrious resident, Muriel Beadle.[7] She pointed out that the purpose of her article was to identify the trials that that community had already suffered so that other communities could learn from them. In describing the turmoil brought about by divergent group pressures and values within the community, she wrote: "The local answer has been that integration cannot succeed unless the class level and customs of the two groups are approximately equal."[8] She explained that the bitterest pill that the community had had to swallow "was to accept the fact that the stated objectives of conservation and renewal could not be obtained unless (1) the community accepted integration, (2) treated integration as a class problem, and (3) discriminated against lower income families and individuals."[9]

Thus, the population of the area decreased from approximately 76,000 in 1956 to 55,000 in 1966. Concomitantly, the black population decreased from 49 percent in 1960 to approximately 38 percent in 1966--because most poor black families were forced to move out. Beadle said that, while Hyde Park had accepted a small proportion of public housing projects, they had been small units that were "low rise in character and scattered to prevent 'downgrading' of community."[10]

Beadle feels that the results to date, after many years of community struggle, are good race relations, although there is not, and doubtless will never be, a balanced racial mixture on the block. She pointed out that, while all seventeen census tracts in the 1960 census include blacks and whites, the percentages varied from 99 percent white in one to 96 percent black in another. She wrote further that "balancing this pattern of housing is an uncommon amount of joint usage, by all races, of community facilities and of joint participation in community activities."[11]

Beadle also discussed the costs associated with this community-wide undertaking. Naturally, the cost in community volunteer time is difficult, if not impossible, to calculate. However, she stipulated that, by the time the "books" were closed, there were more than $46 million of expenditures in public funds and $250 million in private funds invested in the two square-mile area over a five-year period. This includes the $29 million expenditure by the University of Chicago. To date, the university invests $300,000 per year for private police to protect the area. This expenditure has proved to be most effective: The crime rate has dropped 50 percent, with the result that this area now boasts of one of the city's lowest crime rates.

The three remaining projects have not been discussed in detail because of the scanty information on them.

These are classified as "other" and "no answer" in
Table 26. However, it is important to point out
that the River Acres-Mt. Clemens, Michigan, project
was the only nomination that claimed to be a successful example of class integration. The community,
which is 95 percent black, is said to contain a mix
of welfare, blue collar, white collar, and professional households.

CONCLUSIONS DRAWN FROM
THE NATIONAL SURVEY

While making no claim that the national survey
is exhaustive and, therefore, realizing that it is
possible for us be ignorant about some existing success stories, the findings have led us to make the
following tentative conclusions:

First, our country currently contains few successful examples of areas integrated in terms of
either race, economic, or sociocultural mix, and the
majority of those that do exist are located in central
cities.

Second, Gruen Gruen + Associates survey was not
able to uncover a single example of an area that
consists of a successful three-way integration. Thus,
for example, the only area that claimed success in
mixing households of different classes was a primarily black community. Two of the projects that
had achieved a stabilized racial integration did so
partially by the process of expelling the lowest-
income residents through slum clearance projects.
In addition, all areas that have achieved a stable
racial mix have had to control the proportion of
minority households.

Third, the mixing of structural units appears
to be the easiest mix to achieve. There are nine
areas that provide a mixture of single-family and
apartment-dwelling unit options. However, many of
these refer to the efforts that have been taken to
control the attractiveness of the area.

Fourth, the most successfully integrated areas have had active and powerful community organizations, which work to provide a safe, harmonious, and attractive environment, with special emphasis given to the protection and improvement of the school system.

Fifth, the most successful projects are those in which residential self-selection has played a prominent part. This is, of course, particularly relevant for higher-income residents, who have numerous other housing opportunities.

Sixth, this survey includes no successful example of mixed communities that are integrated on a social relationship, rather than a physical nexus basis. Despite the efforts of community organizations to sponsor "get-together" activities, these activities are generally conducted on a formal basis and have not led to widespread informal friendship relationships.

NOTES

1. Muriel Beadle, "The Hyde Park-Kenwood Urban Renewal Years, A History to Date," Private Printing 25.

2. Post (Denver), May 3, 1970.

3. Ibid.

4. Ibid.

5. Ibid.

6. Mayor's Committee for Community Renewal, "Integrated Housing in the Lafayette-Elmwood Area," (Detroit: 1970), p. 4.

7. Beadle, op. cit.

8. Ibid., p. 18.

9. Ibid., p. 17.

10. *Ibid*., p. 19.

11. *Ibid*., p. 20.

8

WHAT
WILL WORK

". . . as far as I'm concerned, a policy
that involved forced integration of the
suburbs or racial balance would fail; that
it's not a sound policy; and this department is not undertaking a policy of racial
balance or racial quotas or forced integration, or anything of that character."*

DIRECTIONS FOR SOLUTIONS

The research and analysis conducted during the
past nine months was aimed at exposing the complex
factors that prevent the housing programs that assist
financially limited households from being used any-
where but in older central city neighborhoods. It
was also the hope of the MVRPC that the work done by
us would indicate directions for finding solutions
to this problem. It is believed by us that the results
of this study do this--that they point to solutions
that, if implemented, will benefit the occupants of
the new housing, the suburban communities in which
the new units will be located, and the quality of
housing available to all the residents of the region.

---

*George Romney, Secretary of HUD, at a press
conference, November 25, 1970.

The directions that were received came from
several sources. The low- and moderate-income households that were interviewed provided guidelines by
describing their needs. This knowledge not only
pointed to some clear directions, but suggested some
that would not aggravate suburbanites' fears, which
could inhibit the program. The suburban responses
summarized in Chapters 3 and 4 suggested another set
of guidelines that must be followed, directions that,
as indicated in Chapter 5, the suburbanites have also
given to their public officials.

Further guidelines are provided by the urban
experiences cited in Chapter 6, which indicate the
type of dangers that must be prevented if the effects
that the suburbanites fear are to be forestalled.
In that chapter, there was also an attempt to point
out the critical, social and economic factors that
interrelate, to determine the impact of expanding
low- and moderate-income housing opportunities into
the suburbs. The MVRPC already has completed a
series of housing component studies that enable it
to appraise the present state of these factors in
the region.

If the knowledge gained from these various
sources is acted upon, it can be expanded into solutions through programs that combine action with a
continuing monitoring of relevant factors. The
direction drawn from the research will be described
below. The evaluation of the existing tools or
federal housing programs in terms of their ability
to be used to take action in the indicated direction
and the suggestions concerning needed new tools are
presented in Chapter 9.

The responsibility and resources for taking
the required action must be placed in the hands of
the MVRPC and the public agencies it works with on
local, state, and federal levels. These guidelines
cannot merely be turned over to the private housing
"delivery system." This is said not because that
system is felt to be either inadequate or unwilling--
quite the contrary: The real estate brokers, housing
contractors, land developers, bankers, and mortgage

brokers who were approached in the course of this
study indicated that the construction industry was
not impeded by complex social or political motives.
They build housing when it is profitable for them to
do so, and this is true whether or not the resultant
product meets the following directions or criteria.

A Wide Variety of Structural
and Locational Options

There is a tendency for all of us to lump those
who differ from us into a single, undifferentiated
group. This is especially true of those who have
less money than we do. In the time of Charles
Dickens, those at the bottom of the economic ladder
were frequently called "the undeserving poor"; today,
they tend to be categorized as "the deserving poor."
Neither categorization is useful because it implies
a uniformity of preferences and life styles that
does not exist or because it suggests the disastrous
and ridiculous notion that these people should live
in the manner prescribed by someone else.

The low- and moderate-income sample that was
interviewed had very definite preferences for the
various structural types that were shown to it. The
suburban respondents were shown the same set of
pictures and were asked to say how they felt such
buildings would fit into their neighborhoods and
communities. Some of the structural types that were
liked by many of the low- and moderate-income households were disliked by many of the higher-income
suburbanites. But there were several types that
were acceptable to both. Thus, if these interviews
had been used to suggest the kind of structures that
should actually be designed and built, it would have
been possible to select structural types that satisfy
both those who will live in, and next to, the new
units. The programs under which the units would
actually be built should also offer such a selection.

The low- and moderate-income households that
were interviewed differed dramatically in where they
preferred to live. Many, as indicated earlier,

wanted to stay in their old neighborhoods or at least
to live in a socially familiar environment, while
others wanted to move into the suburbs. Some could
benefit economically from such facilities as child
care centers. The majority wanted to live in neighborhoods with those of their own class, but to share
community facilities with members of other socioeconomic classes. A minority wanted to live scattered
among the existing suburban residential neighborhoods,
with neighbors of higher income. But, most significantly, those who picked this option tended to be in
the moderate-income group and to have characteristics
that suggested they are or would be upwardly mobile
and wanted to conform to the standards of such neighborhoods.

     Thus, only a wide variety of locational options
could serve the divergent needs of those who will
need assistance to buy or rent new housing. The
availability of many possible options would also be
much more likely to permit the selection of options
that meet the needs of low- and moderate-income
households without creating the effects that the
suburbanites fear. There should be a maximum number
of possible choices.

Eventual Home Ownership Generally
Preferable to Continued Renting

     Home ownership is a goal of most low- and
moderate-income households. Several studies suggest,
in addition to the regional survey, that the greatest
benefit and incentive for upward mobility that can
be provided by any environmental factor is home
ownership in a compatible neighborhood. The suburbanites also prefer seeing owneroccupied housing in
their areas. The criterion of ownership appears to
be particularly important in the Miami Valley region,
which contrasts with many coastal cities in its
relatively low proportion of highly mobile executives.
This region's negative attitude toward the renter may
alter as the region experiences more mobility of the
executive class and as larger numbers of its wealthier
citizens seek luxury apartment residences. However,

wherever possible, ownership opportunities should be
pursued. If home ownership is not feasible, then
the ownership of an apartment unit should be pursued,
since it would provide many of the same psychic
benefits.

Viable Class Mix Necessary to Preserve
Neighborhood Stability

Attempts should be made to establish a viable
class mix on the neighborhood level. A viable mix
would be one that permits and provides the opportunity
for voluntary class integration on this level. Thus,
those who want to live with households of differing
classes could do so. However, extreme class heterogeneity should not be imposed on a neighborhood
level. Not one of the suburbanites or representatives
of the low- and moderate-income households that was
interviewed wanted to live in extremely class- heterogeneous neighborhoods. If such heterogeneity is
imposed on a neighborhood level, it is likely to
produce friction, with the more affluent classes
eventually moving out and failing to move in. Much
wider degrees of class heterogeneity will be accepted
within a community than within a neighborhood without
inducing instability. The only likely exceptions to
this neighborhood rule would involve situations where
the less well-to-do classes form a conforming and
permanently small minority. However, extremely broad
"social balance" should be sought at the community,
not neighborhood, level.

Informing, Counseling, and Directing Low
and Moderate Income Households Toward
Appropriate Housing Environments

A well-trained and informed staff will be needed
to properly accomplish the placement of lower-income
housing in the suburbs. Those who are eligible for
the housing must be informed of the options available
to them. This task cannot be left only to the
developers of subsidized units. Many of those eligible
will have no previous experience with purchasing real

estate or making rental arrangements outside of the
central city. Therefore, they will need "buyer's
agents" to help them bargain with experienced sellers
and rental agents and also to make sure that they
fully comprehend the financial and maintenance responsibilities they must assume.

The needed counseling and informing agency should
also become involved in the job of matching housing
options to household capabilities and in monitoring
the results of various matchings. There should be
a feedback over time, so that future development can
be improved to better serve the low-/moderate-income
households. The initial placement should be based
on the housing needs of those placed and their
capabilities to adjust well in the new environment.
Such placement should never serve as a substitute
for needed social or psychological therapy.

Housing Packages and Support Programs That
    Meet Requirements of Low and Moderate
Income Groups and Older Suburban Residents

This study suggests that suburban communities
will accept programs that expand low- and moderate-
income housing opportunities if the suburban features
that they now enjoy are safeguarded and improved.
This means that the housing "packages" must be
developed within a framework of programs that assist
financially limited families and individuals to pay
for, or rent, new dwelling units, while simultaneously
assisting the community facilities that will be
called on to serve the nonhousing needs of the residents.

The facilitating programs should include the
following:

1. Provisions to give the lower-income occupants
the resources and incentives for, or other guarantees
of, property maintenance

2. Support to preclude the imposition of tax
burdens or pressures for service reductions upon the
suburban community

3. Support to preclude a drop in the quality
of the local schools

4. Provisions for any additionally needed
public services, such as child care centers and youth
programs, and health, fire, and police personnel.

Credible Programs To Preserve and
Enhance the Suburban Environment

The Miami Valley Regional Housing Plan is an
unusually well-documented and -prepared regional
housing plan. Even more unusual, however, is the
fact that the elected officials who represent their
communities on the MVRPC approved the plan in a
community-by-community roll call vote. Twenty-six
commissioners voted for the resolution, two abstained,
and none voted against the plan. Some representatives
voted affirmatively, in spite of the fact that many
of their constituents were hostile to the housing
plan and, particularly, its target allocation of low-
and moderate-income households to the suburbs. These
commissioners voted for the plan in the belief that
its implementation could be accomplished in a way
that would not only provide the region with a more
beneficial development pattern but also work to
benefit their own communities.

For very practical reasons the implementation
of the plan must keep faith with their belief. The
housing product includes physical and social elements
that provide shelter and a host of psychological
benefits. In one sense, housing is much like romance:
Expectations strongly influence our perceptions of
the experience. The fact that many present residents
of the suburban Miami Valley fear that some negative
results will follow the entry of additional low- and
moderate- income households into their communities
increases the likelihood of adverse effects. Thus,
the efforts to preserve and enhance the suburban
environment must be effective. If they are, subsequent
efforts in the Miami Valley and elsewhere will be
more easily accomplished. If such initial efforts
should fail, it will become increasingly difficult
to find the opportunity to try again.

CHAPTER

9

**EXISTING PROGRAMS
AND RECOMMENDATIONS
FOR
INCREASED
SUBURBAN HOUSING**

"Why, after the battle is over and the
people are in . . . well, you know, nobody
pays any attention. It works. It really
does work."[1]

PROGRAMS AND CRITERIA

In the previous chapter, directions or criteria
for use in conceptualizing and evaluating solutions
to the problem of placing lower-income housing in
suburban middle-income neighborhoods and communities
were presented. In this chapter, these criteria are
used to evaluate the federal programs that can help
to provide such housing and to suggest the kind of
program augmentations that seem necessary.

Federal housing aids to upper- and middle-income
Americans come in such subtle and indirect forms as
tax benefits, mortgage market manipulations, and
public capital improvement grants. The assistance
that is available to low- and moderate-income households from HUD and the Department of Agriculture is
much more direct. It includes loans and grants to
local public housing agencies, rent supplements,
mortgage payment subsidies, and below-market mortgage
interest loans. These subsidies are provided under
a myriad of existing programs, but pending legislation

will probably consolidate them into a few broad,
basic authorities. These subsidies have been grouped
into four basic types of programs.

    The first type of program provides rental units
delivered by local public housing agencies in conformity with the oldest form of low-income assistance--
public housing. The overwhelming majority of these
units are in central cities. While most have been
built with federal loans and are owned and operated
by the local public housing authority, increasing
use has been made of a 1965 congressional authoriza-
tion for local housing authorities to lease existing
private houses and to buy new units under the turnkey
method. Under the leasing programs, the federal
government makes up the difference between the cost
of the lease and the amount paid by the low-income
tenant. Such leased public housing remains on the
public tax roles, even though it receives federal
subsidy.

    Under the turnkey method of building units for
public housing, the local housing authority contracts
with private builders to buy, upon completion, housing
they have built or rehabilitated. Any builder with
a suitable site or structure can approach the local
authority with a proposal to build or rehabilitate
in accordance with his own plans. If the offer is
accepted, the authority buys the units upon their
completion. The turnkey approach can also be applied
to the management of low-rent housing projects under
a program by which rental projects are operated by
a private management firm or by a tenant organization.

    The second program type is that of public housing
ownership. In recent years, HUD has also been allowing
local housing agencies to provide lease-purchase
rights to low-income families. This is the case,
for example, under Turnkey III, a program made
possible by Section 59 of the 1965 Housing Act.
Local housing authorities are also authorized to sell
some of their low-rent units to tenants.

    In this analysis, public housing has been split
into rental and ownership categories, though both

can be built publicly or privately or administered
initially by private firms or the local public
agency. Furthermore, both can receive federal grants
for counseling and to provide other tenant services.
Of course, in all cases, the programs cannot be used
locally unless money is available, and one of the
reasons for our presentation of the following evaluation is to help local decision-makers to select the
type of program for whose funding they are prepared
to fight.

The third category of housing program types
groups those programs that subsidize nonpublicly
owned rental housing made available to lower-income
households at rents that do not exceed 25 percent
of the household's income. These subsidies come in
two forms. The form that is now most common is that
provided under Section 236. This program, authorized
under the Housing and Urban Development Act of 1968,
provides assistance in the form of periodic payment
to the mortgagee, financing the housing to reduce
the mortgager's interest costs on a market rate
FHA-insured project. The mortgager must be a non-
profit organization, a cooperative, or a private
limited dividend entity. However, the reader should
not presume that this means that all developers or
owners of a 236 project are acting out of pure
altruism--the combination of low-interest mortgage
and U.S. tax laws allows the owner to achieve good
returns, even if the cash dividend is limited. This
same category includes programs that supplement the
rent of low-income families living in the projects
receiving the mortgage payment assistance. These
supplements are available to elderly and handicapped
low-income households or those displaced by government action.

Home ownership assistance programs make up the
final category of available tools. The Housing and
Urban Redevelopment Act of 1968 authorizes Section
235 to provide for mortgage payment subsidies to
lower the monthly payment of moderate-income households.

A subjective evaluation of these four types of

programs is presented here, to indicate the criteria
for programs that will work to open up suburban
housing opportunities. The evaluation was based, in
part, on published descriptions of the federal
programs. An exhaustive and quantitative evaluative
study of the existing federal programs was not made,
though the overview suggests that this would be a
most worthwhile project to fund. However, face-to-
face and telephone interviews were conducted with
lenders, builders, developers, and housing "packagers"
in the Miami Valley region in order to have the
benefit of their knowledge and experience. For each
criterion, high, low, or median grades have been
assigned to each program for the reasons discussed
below.

Wide Variety of Structural and
Locational Possibilities

Theoretically, the housing provided under the
rental and public housing programs may be of any
structural type--high-rise, garden apartment, row
houses, semidetached, or detached. Actually, cost
not only limits the design features that can be
included but, even more importantly, tends to create
pressures for relatively high-density projects.
Builders in the Dayton area also complained that the
Housing Assistance Administration (HAA) standards
for turnkey housing were excessively high and that
costs were increased because of these standards and
the need to visit Chicago in order to get specifications approved. These turnkey builders had been used
to working with the FHA office in Cincinnati and
preferred FHA regulations and the convenience of a
nearby office. The proximity problem should be
reduced when HUD locates their Ohio office in
Columbus in line with their anticipated reorganization.

The locations that are available to the builder
of public housing are limited to those areas that
are served by a public housing authority. This
excludes a very large proportion of the region,
including all of Miami County, Preble County, and
Darke County. Greene County has a public authority,

the Yellow Springs Housing Authority, which has
recently been expanded to serve the entire county.
Only Montgomery County, served by the DMHA, has
received a significant number of public housing units.
The fact that only leased public housing units pay
their full share of local property taxes, while the
remainder only make payments in lieu of taxes, also
works to keep some areas from signing local cooperation agreements. Thus, the public housing program
has been given a low to medium grade on this criterion.

The 235 home ownership program was given a
medium to high score. More localities are willing
to accept this program, because the units constructed
under it are difficult to distinguish from the
ubiquitous moderate-income single-family tract home
and because the program is for moderate- rather than
low-income households. Because they attract renters
rather than owners, the 236 projects have found more
resistance than 235, but not nearly as much as public
housing. While this is, to some extent, a subjective
evaluation, the design quality of existing 235 and
236 projects appears quite variable and depends
primarily on the individual builder. Builders of
the 235 and 236 programs are given more leeway than
those building under public housing programs. Unfortunately, there is little positive design control
imposed on these programs by competition. Therefore,
rental housing was given a medium grade, while the
ownership private programs were given a medium to
high grade on the criterion of possible structural
and locational variety. In all cases, of course,
locational restrictions are more likely to come
because of local attitudes about expected impacts
than because of the specific features of the housing
programs.

Eventual Home Ownership Possible

This criterion is, of course, only met by two
of the four program types. In the long run, this
may mean that programs such as 236 and standard
public housing may be restricted to the elderly and
those households who cannot adjust to, or do not
want to live in, their own home.

Viable Class Mix

Rental public housing programs earn a low score
on this criterion. The fact that a family must leave
these projects when its income climbs to 125 percent
of entrance requirements tends to make these projects
the exclusive domain of those with little or no class
mobility. Rental housing (236) earns a medium score,
because it does not force occupants to leave as
their incomes increase--it merely raises the rents.

In some cases, it was told to us that wives had
left their jobs in order to qualify for 235 or 236
housing. If this is true, the programs are not
motivating households in the manner Congress expected.
Furthermore, local and national data suggests that
black moderate-income families are less likely to
be served by the 235 program than white moderate-
income families. Instead, this program seems to be
attracting a high proportion of young white households, while black households seem more likely to be
served by the 235J program, which subsidizes the
rehabilitation and sale of older units. One reason
for this is, of course, the previously indicated
racial bias one finds in the suburbs where more of
the new units are being built. Another reason deals
with the way information about the availability of
these units in disseminated. (This second issue is
discussed below.) However, these limitations also
affect the opportunities for racial mix obtainable
under the 235 program.

Also, relatively few 235 units have been built
as Planned Unit Developments. They have tended,
rather, to be included in tract development merely
catering to those households with slightly less
income than the families that can obtain standard
Section 203 FHA mortgages. If Planned Unit Development techniques were used more frequently, as in the
case of the Seattle "Choice" project, then a wider
range of income groups could be served, as some of
the units could be priced lower than is otherwise
the case, even with the mortgage subsidy.

Informing and Counseling
Potential Users

The rental public housing programs probably de-
serve medium scores on the criterion of informing
potential users about the programs' availability and
counseling tenants. The DMHA staff does work with
tenants on a continuing basis. In areas where Turnkey
III public housing ownership programs are available,
this program gets a high mark. In a telephone conversation with us, Dorothy Duke, member of the National Council of Negro Women, when discussing the $33
million in Turnkey III Public Housing she helped
establish in 1968, 1969, and, 1970, said: "You can't
just do a structure without providing supportive
services." She seems to have gotten the funding
required to provide these services, including counseling.

There is a counseling program (237) for home
owners listed in the federal statutes, but no instances of such counseling actually being funded by
the federal government were found. Generally, the
235 program is sold by the private builder to who-
ever comes to see his development. In several cases
that were told to us, the procedure is very simple.
If a prospect who comes into the development cannot
meet standard credit terms, he is turned over to a
salesman who understands the paperwork requirements
of 235. If the prospect appears to be eligible, the
paperwork is processed. He receives no counseling,
except by the salesman. If he can meet the obligation
of a home owner--fine; if not, that will become
apparent later.

The 236 program offers no counseling, nor is
there any effort made to direct central city residents
who could benefit and qualify to existing projects.
There are, of course, exceptions to this, particularly
in the case of projects built especially for the
elderly.

Resources and Incentives for Maintenance

The DMHA has done a well-above-average job of maintaining its units and working with tenants to prevent unnecessary destruction. However, the average rental public housing projects are running into serious trouble in trying to preserve the quality of their units. A study of operating costs in public housing projects across the country found their maintenance costs rising so quickly that the report was subtitled "A Financial Crisis."[2] While the rising costs have forced many local public housing authorities to rise rents, Frank deLeeuw's study suggests that rents have not kept pace with the increases. He concludes that "growing deficits seem by far the most likely short-run outcome."[3] Thus, rental public housing programs will probably experience increasing difficulty in the maintenance area, unless local authorities take special care to prevent this eventuality.

The problem of providing incentives to encourage occupants to help hold down maintenance and repair expenses is particularly acute for rental public housing units. On the other hand, when the possibility for home ownership is tied to successful efforts to minimize operating costs, a very real incentive is provided. As mentioned in the previous chapter, the state of Hawaii reports great success with programs that put the money saved on operating costs into a pool that then provides down payment for the occupant of the well and inexpensively kept units.

Turnkey III programs have similar incentives; further, if provided with adequate support programs, they have a guarantee of needed resources should a financial disaster strike the occupied households. The importance of this point should not be understated, since the household who cannot afford market housing assuredly cannot afford to weather the "unusual" repair bill that sooner or later faces all home owners.

The 236 programs are given a medium rating because, while the tenants usually have no particular incentive to maintain the property, the landlord does.

If the property runs down, his resale opportunities will be lessened.

The 235 program was rated low to high on this criterion, since the reports that were obtained suggested that much depended on the attitudes of the occupant; no uniform screening was applied to keep out households that would not maintain the property. Several lenders pointed out that some 235 occupants were young households with no equity in the units and that some gave little evidence of respecting their obligations as home owners. Thus, these lenders worried that careless budgeting habits and indifference might lead to undermaintenance. On the other hand, several builders told us that the 235 units they sold were going to couples who took pride in their homes and "were keeping them up properly."

An Even Ratio of Tax Payments to Public Service Requirements

All public housing programs were given a low to medium grade on the subject of tax-to-service-cost ratios. There are, of course, many elderly occupants of public housing units who cause the property taxpayers little expense. But, generally, the in lieu payment made by the public housing authority probably does not cover the full costs of the local public services required by tenants. Leased public housing does pay property taxes.

Privately built rental units (236) were awarded medium to high grades. They pay property taxes and, at least in the Miami Valley region, tend not to have large numbers of children requiring public services. The 235 program gets a medium grade, because, while residents pay property taxes, they typically do have children.

Preserving School Quality

None of the programs has any special provisions enabling it to deal specifically with the problems

of preserving school quality. Those that keep the
units on the property tax rolls will tend to contribute
more to the school bill than those who do not. Thus,
the scores here are similar to those that were awarded
for the general criterion dealing with the ratio of
taxes paid to local services used. However, this is
clearly a matter that should be carefully evaluated
on a case-by-case basis.

The problem raised by the fact that public
housing does not pay its full share of property taxes
was introduced by an earlier study of the impact of
public housing upon the school systems within the
Miami Valley region. This study concludes:

> It is our opinion that concurrent with the
> acceptance of a limited number of Public
> Housing units in each School District, we
> must seek State or Federal legislation to
> eliminate the apparent burden than Public
> Housing will unevenly present to the School
> District.[4]

Providing for Additionally
Needed Public Services

The arrival of low- and moderate-income households into the suburbs may require extra services
to guarantee their beneficial absorption into the
suburban community. Some of these facilities, such
as child care centers, are sometimes provided under
the Turnkey III or 236 programs, but even this is
not universal. Such broader needs as extra youth
programs or additional health, fire, and police
personnel are not directly contemplated in any of
the programs. Therefore, all the existing programs
were given a low score on this criterion.

Credibility in Terms of Ability
To Preserve and Enhance the
Suburban Environment

The credibility of each program depends upon its
actual ability to satisfy the previous four criteria,

if necessary, and the expectations of the suburbanites
concerning this ability. As the subjective evaluations indicate, no program fulfills all the criteria,
since each lacks some of the needed capabilities and
can only deal with specific situations under certain
conditions. However, virtually all of them can be
effectively used to preserve and to enhance the
suburban environment under some conditions, particularly if used or packaged with other available
programs.

Thus, for example, the 235 program is working
quite well, particularly in situations where the
developer definitely maintains a fixed relatively
low quota of such subsidized units within a development made up primarily of regular FHA or convention-
ally insured nonsubsidized units. However, even
such projects could run into trouble if the school
system were already at capacity or if some tenants
could not or would not keep up maintenance. Furthermore, only a portion of the needed housing can be
built within nonsubsidized developments.

There are examples of existing housing programs
serving the housing and living environment needs of
the low-income without violating the attractions of
the existing milieu. Unfortunately, there are many
less positive examples, some of which have had wide
publicity--for instance, the high-rise public housing
projects in Chicago. Unfortunately, all existing
programs lack the ability to add extra public services
if required, or to deal directly with the need to
preserve school quality.

The Miami Valley Regional Housing Plan calls
for 14,125 new housing units to be built in the
suburbs, or an addition of approximately 7 percent
to the existing housing stock. A proportion of these
can be built with the existing housing programs if
carefully located. However, if wide-scale housing
opportunities are to be offered, those who cannot
afford market housing, then efforts must be made to
find additional funding sources to provide the backup
to these housing programs.

The initial attempts are crucial, since,

unfortunately, future expectations concerning the
programs will drop if some of the early attempts
fail. Many of the people surveyed are already particularly fearful of any public housing programs. Credibility depends on the specific set of programs and
the manner in which they are implemented. Therefore,
it was not possible to give subjective scores to the
four broadly grouped programs relative to this
criterion.

NEEDED ANCILLARY PROGRAMS TO PROTECT
AND IMPROVE THE STATUS QUO

     Most of the programs subjectively evaluated
above were designed to enable a private party non-
profit group or local public housing authority to
provide housing for those without the means to buy
or rent elsewhere. They were not designed to open
up new suburban locations to groups that now live
mainly in the central cities or in the older rural
and urban fringe neighborhoods that are geographically
in the suburbs but were built before recent periods
of "suburbanization." Therefore, it is not surprising
that these governmental aids to the building and
operation of housing fail to provide the added measures
of community protection that are sometimes needed
if such housing is not to alter the features that
attract and hold the present residents of the suburbs
where it is placed.

     Unless ancillary programs or institutions are
used to protect these attractive suburban features,
the present residents will resist the entry of new
classes into the suburbs. This resistance will
strengthen as one moves down the economic class scale
in attempts to provide direct housing. As has been
mentioned before, the suburbanite's willingness to
accept the new households will diminish if he sees
examples of decline in environmental quality as a
result of the new housing.

     The fact that ancillary programs are needed to
open up the suburbs to new classes should be no
surprise to anyone familiar with the processes of

development that brought the present residents of the
suburbs to their homes. These residents were not only
helped by the FHA programs that have insured more
than $130 billion in mortgages and assisted more than
9.5 million families to become home owners and enabled
more than 1.4 million apartments to be built. They
were also aided by federal and state programs that
built roads into the suburbs and paid for significant
essential portions of the public infrastructure,
such as sewage and water plants. The developers
who turned raw land into middle- and upper-income
neighborhoods may have fought with the city planners,
public work officials, and other officials who imposed zoning laws, building codes, and other regulations upon them. But these officials also worked
to bring up utility lines and roads to the edge of
the developer's site. Perhaps even more importantly,
the restrictions they managed to impose and the
public facilities they provided made it easier for
subsequent developers to build and profitably sell
middle- and upper-income houses.

If the initial efforts to build low- and moderate-income housing in the suburbs are to succeed
and lead to further successes, they must be made in
concert with other programs and institutions that
will maintain or raise community service levels and
help to make the suburbs more desirable in the future.
This subjective evaluation of programs suggests that,
under certain situations, the following areas will
need more programmatic or institutional protection
and improvement than will be provided by the existing
housing programs:

School Quality

Educational quality can be threatened if the
property taxes generated by the new units do not
provide the added funds needed to serve the children
of the new households. The same possibility exists
with the entry of middle-income families with children. The problem is caused primarily by our being
reliant on the local property tax to support the
local school district.

There are several ways that this threat could
be eliminated. One method that appeals to us would
be to test the utility of the frequently discussed
educational voucher systems with a federal program
that gives such vouchers to the low- and moderate-
income families who move into the new suburban units.
The voucher would be equal in value to the appropriate
cost of educating a pupil in the average local
school system, but the parent would be free to give
the money to the school system of his choice. That
is, he could give it to the local school system or
enroll his children in a private school, giving them
the voucher in payment for tuition. Such an approach
would not only permit the federal government to test
a program that it has already agreed to test somewhere,
but it would also offer the possibility of unusual
cash gains to the local school systems if they adapt
to the needs of their new pupils, while maintaining
quality education for all.

An alternate solution to this problem was recently put forth by the California Statewide Council
on Long-Range School Finance Planning. It suggests
that the state collect a certain amount of property
tax from all school districts and then return the
money to the local districts in proportion to their
student load. Such a system would distribute the
property tax receipts available for education among
all students in the state, thus freeing educational
quality from its ties to the local property tax base.

Added General Public And
Special Service

Although there is a variety of federal and state
social aid programs, these are not coordinated with
the housing programs under discussion here. This
is true of general public service programs, such as
health and law enforcement. If such programs were
known to be available if needed, the resulting effect
on expectations would tend to reduce the amount of
such services that would actually be required.
Conversely, the knowledge that needed public services
probably will not be augmented until the local

capacities have been obviously strained will tend to
encourage and even magnify local concern.

Even such a necessary service as counseling for
the new occupants is rarely provided in conjunction
with the housing programs. The sellers and renters
of units who do give such services are also not
always the best equipped to do so. Finally, special
programs that would apply to all low- and moderate-
income subsidized suburban units are rarely available,
even when they would make the housing programs much
more acceptable. Thus, for example, there is no
program to specially inspect and deal with maintenance
problems; yet, the existence of a guarantee of good
maintenance would be extremely beneficial.

NEED FOR ANOTHER KIND OF
HOUSING PROGRAM

All of the programs that have been subjectively
evaluated can be used under various conditions to
build a housing project or a limited number of houses.
The federal government has also authorized a program
that provides support for developers seeking to build
new towns. There is a noticeable gap between the
scale of development envisioned for the programs
that have been evaluated and for the new town legis-
lation--a gap that might be termed "the minineighbor-
hood." Programs to facilitate the construction of
such minineighborhoods would be an extremely valuable
additional tool for those willing to provide expanded
suburban housing opportunities for low- and moderate-
income households. These minineighborhoods would
be less expensive to build than new towns because
they could share elements of the existing suburban
infrastructure that are not yet operating at full
capacity. Furthermore, it is often cheaper to add
to existing community facilities and services than
to attempt to provide all new facilities and services.

Minineighborhoods could construct new elementary
schools and child care centers to serve their own
neighborhood needs but share the high school and
other facilities of the larger community of which

they are a part.   Thus, the program being suggested
would aid in the construction and operation of the
elementary school and the placement of neighborhood
roads and utilities. A variety of options, now
foreclosed, would then be open. For example, the
older, run-down sections West Dayton contain many
blocks inhabited partly by low- to moderate-income
households who have the capacity for home ownership
and the development of a sound community spirit.
These residents now have only the options of moving
separately into a neighborhood environment that is
foreign to them or rehabilitating their older houses.
The new program that is suggested by us would enable
these present neighbors to band together, should
they so desire, and live in new houses in a new
neighborhood, without breaking old social ties.

IMPLEMENTATION

The programmatic and institutional deficiencies
summarized above should be corrected if the open
land of the suburbs is to be used to grant new housing
opportunities to low- and moderate-income Americans
capable of grasping such opportunities. However,
even if all the deficiencies that have been noted
are corrected, a significant number of opportunities
will not result unless the various programs are
combined to provide maximum benefit to the region's
low- and moderate-income households and the suburban
communities in which they locate. Individual builders
may utilize the programs to produce housing but they
lack the information and the resources required to
best serve the full spectrum of those who need such
housing or to deal comprehensively with the impact
of this housing on the suburbs. To do this on the
required scale, the builders and developers will
need help and guidance. Programs must be selected
and evaluated in the field in terms of their ability
to contribute to the continued expansion of suburban
housing opportunities for all segments of the population. It will not be easy for an implementing body
to follow the directions outlined in the previous
chapter. Clearly, the implementing group must have
a regional and long-range perspective, while it

simultaneously perceives and deals with the needs of
the newer low- and moderate-income residents of the
suburbs and the real problems and fears imposed upon
the older, more affluent suburbanites. This will
not be easy. The temptation to become an advocate
for one group or the other will be great. If this
temptation is not resisted, good efforts will be
undermined.

   Those who will occupy the new units may need
social, occupational, and financial counseling.
They also need to be listened to, so that the housing
and other services they require can be continually
improved. As stressed above, these new households
will have an impact on the suburbs in which they
are located. These communities do not need an
implementing agency to propagandize them about the
beneficial aspects of this impact. Instead, they
need an implementer that can foresee and, hence,
forestall problems. They also need an implementer
to monitor these impacts on a continuing basis or,
failing that, to recognize unanticipated problems
so that they can be dealt with quickly and effectively.
The implementing agency should do more than disseminate
information and advise how desired housing can come
into being. It should also work with local planning
agencies to use the traditional tools of land use
planning to encourage the construction of developments
and units that would benefit both the resident and
the community and guard against projects that would
tend to deteriorate the community's quality.

   This implementing agency can only perform its
function if it maintains current and accurate
information about the factors in the urban environment that are of concern to all its residents. We
have tried to report here on the factors that are
important to the potential occupants and the present
suburbanites of the Miami Valley region. Existing
attitudes have been cataloged. There is a great
need to maintain current data on what is happening
in those communities. Little will be gained if the
basic information that has been developed by the
MVRPC as it prepared its housing element is merely
used to suggest that all subsequent actions will

automatically go well. This point is emphasized
because our nationwide questioning elicited some
enthusiastic descriptions of situations, both good
and bad, that turned out to lack any supporting
evidence.

Thus, for example, one implementer of a housing
integration program told us that racial and class
integration was working very well in his neighborhood.
He had not been included in the survey, but it was
of interest to us to find out if the area he mentioned
should be included. It was decided not to include
it after he consistently was unable to answer specifically any questions about the state of the relevant
factors in his neighborhood. He knew that things
were going well, but he could not say how many
families had moved in or out or what their composition
was. He knew that the assessor who had told us that
property values were declining in the neighborhood
was wrong, but he had no data on sales prices or the
nature of shifts in the effective demand for housing
or housing quality.

This example is cited merely to emphasize the
fact that goodwill alone will not bring about effective implementation. However, if state and federal
support is provided, the kind of information that
the MVRPC has been collecting can be used to permit
the accomplishment of the stated goals. The information in this study is presented as a needed addition
to that stock.

The MVRPC is the most logical candidate to act
as the implementing agency in this region. At a
minimum, this agency could evaluate proposed projects
in terms of the criteria that apply both to their
ability to meet the needs of the particular low- and
moderate-income households that are to live in them
and their ability to mesh beneficially into the
suburban environment. Each proposed new set of
dwelling units should be evaluated, and the following
types of questions asked:

1. Do site and dwelling designs meet the life
style needs of those who are to move into the units,

and do they fit the standards of the area's present residents?

2. Are "buyers' agents" or counselors available to help the new residents make their home purchase or tenancy arrangements?

3. Are the needed public services required by the new residents, such as transportation, child care centers, and job training or other services, available?

4. Have guarantees of maintenance been provided?

5. Have arrangements been made to keep the new complex from increasing the local tax burden or lowering the quality of local services?

6. Have local school officials been contacted and steps taken to assure the preservation of school quality?

No one set of programs can provide positive answers to each of these questions in all cases. Consider, for example, the problems that will be encountered in seeing to it that each group of new suburban residents has the transportation required for them to get to jobs and needed services. In some cases, a location near bus lines may be desirable, but, in another case, it may make more sense to provide periodic "limousine" or taxi service to important destinations. A skillful and innovational tailoring of the programs to the many special sub-groups of present and new suburban residents can cause all programs to get higher grades than have been assigned them.

However, the housing needs of the region cannot be fully met by even the most skillful use of existing programs, unless these programs are improved and augmented. The following types of additional tools are needed in order to make suburban housing oppor-tunities a possibility for all those who desire and can utilize such locations.

First, the development of state or federal
school tax equalization programs that actually make
up differences in the assessed valuation of
property tax per pupil in different school districts.
New public housing in the suburbs should pay full
property taxes.

Second, the passage of new federal legislation
to pay for the services that must frequently accompany the new dwelling units if the low- and moderate-
income households are to be beneficially housed in
the suburbs. In addition, programs to develop low-
and moderate-income dwelling units in the suburbs
should tie into the full range of existing federally
supported programs that provide child care centers,
head-start classes and, other services of the type
that need to be provided in conjunction with housing.

Third, the development of maintenance guarantees
and incentive programs.

Fourth, an expansion of housing programs leading
to home ownership.

Fifth, the development of federal programs to
subsidize the construction of minineighborhoods, both
in the suburbs and the central cities. The development of such a program would complement the present
set of subsidized housing and new town legislation,
so as to provide for the needs and preferences of
all the various subgroups of low- and moderate-income
households.

Sixth, funds should be made available so that
efforts to build low- and moderate-income housing
in the suburbs can be monitored. The impact of these
efforts upon the households that live in the new
units and the suburban environment should be objec-
tively recorded, so that problems can be quickly
noted, remedied, and not repeated elsewhere.

NOTES

1. Dorothy Duke, of the National Council of
Negro Women, discussing the $33 million in Turnkey

III Public Housing she helped establish in 1968, 1969, and 1970. Telephone conversation, September 25, 1970.

2. Frank deLeeuw, Operating Costs in Public Housing: A Financial Crisis (Washington, D.C.: The Urban Institute, 1969).

3. Ibid, p. 13.

4. Paul Tipps, "Probable Effect of Public Housing on Selected School Districts" (June, 1969), p. 11.

Interviewer's Name: _____

Time of Day: Before 12:00 noon___ ; 12:01-4:00p.m.___ ; 4:01-___   __(4)
                                        1   2   3

Day of Week: Mon___ ; Tue___ ; Wed___ ; Thu___ ; Fri___ ; Sat___ ; Sun___   __(5)
                       1   2   3   4   5   6   7

Respondent's Neighborhood: _____   __(6)

Respondent lives: Multi-family ____ ; Single-family____   __(7)
    1st call___   1   2
    Call back___

Hello! My name is _____ . I would like to talk with
you about the idea of providing new housing for low and middle
income families in the suburbs outside the central city. This
survey is to find out how you would feel about the idea of living
in the suburbs like Kettering, Vandalia, Jefferson and Washington
Township, et cetera, rather than where you live now.

1. How long have you lived at your present address?   _____ __(8-9)

2 . Counting yourself, how many adults 18 years of age
    and older live in this household?   _____ __(10)

3. How many children from 13-17 live in this household?   _____ __(11)

4. How many children from 7-12 live in this household?   _____ __(12)

5. How many children 6 and under live in this household?   _____ __(13)

6. Do you presently have any expectation of moving? Yes _____   __(14)
    If yes,   1
                                                         No

6a. Do you expect to move to: _____   __(15)
    a) Another dwelling unit within this neighborhood?   2
    b) Another neighborhood within this community?   1
       Specify_____
    c) Another community somewhere else in this region?   2
       Specify_____
    d) Another region?   3
                                                                   4

7. Does your household contain one or more wage earners?
    If yes,   Yes _____   __(16)
                                                     No   1
7a. Please list the name and location of each   2
    person's place of employment:

Relationship of Name of Place Where Location of Place
Employed Person Person is Employed of Employment   Time Zone

_____ _____ _____ _____   __(17)

_____ _____ _____ _____   __(18)

7a. (Cont'd) Name and location of each person's place of
    employment:

Relationship of Employed Person	Name of Place Where Person is Employed	Location of Place of Employment	Time Zone	
_____	_____	_____	_____	__(19)
_____	_____	_____	_____	__(20)

7b. How do the members of your household get to work?
        Number who use the bus   __(21)
        Number who walk   __(22)
        Number who drive their own car   __(23)
        Number who ride in someone else's car   __(24)
        Other (specify)_____ __(25)

8. What social service facilities does your household currently
    use, such as medical clinics, Welfare Department, child care
    centers, Bureau of Unemployment Compensation, et cetera?

        Household does not use any social service facilities.   __(26)

Name of Social Services Utilized by Respondent Households	Location	FREQUENCY OF USE				
		At Least Once A Wk.	At Least Once A Mo.	At Least Once Every Other Mo.	Fewer Than 6 Times A Year	
A. Welfare Dept.	1	2	3	4	5	__(27)
B. Medical Clinic	1	2	3	4	5	__(28)
C. Child Care Fac.	1	2	3	4	5	__(29)
D. Unemp. Bureau	1	2	3	4	5	__(30)
E. Juvenile Court	1	2	3	4	5	__(31)
F. Child Gd. Ctr.	1	2	3	4	5	__(32)
G. Vets. Admin.	1	2	3	4	5	__(33)
H. Dayton Boys Clb	1	2	3	4	5	__(34)
I. Other (specify)						
	1	2	3	4	5	__(35)
	1	2	3	4	5	__(36)
	1	2	3	4	5	__(37)

If household uses one or more social services:

8a. How do the members of your household get to the social
service facilities?

         Number who use the bus   __(38)
         Number who walk   __(39)
         Number who drive own car   __(40)
         Number who ride in someone else's car   __(41)
         Other (specify)_____ __(42)

9. If you had the following two choices, which would you pick: __(43)
          a) A new home in this immediate area
                     or   _____
                                         1
          b) A new home outside the city somewhere
             in the suburbs?
                                      _____
                                       2

          Why?_____   __(44-
                                                           45)

          _____

          _____

          _____

10. If new housing were to be provided in the suburbs, which of
the following three choices would you pick?   __(46)

   a) Living in new low and moderate housing units
      which are not clustered together but scattered
      among the existing suburban residential neigh-
      borhoods? In this situation most of your
      neighbors would have higher incomes.
                                      _____
                                      1

                       or

   b) Living in a separate neighborhood made up of
      new housing units for low and moderate income
      families. The immediate neighborhood would
      be composed of families with roughly the same
      incomes. However, the neighborhood residents
      would use the same community facilities, in-
      cluding schools, used by all other neighbor-
      hoods in the city or township.
                                      _____
                                      2

                       or

   c) Living in a separate neighborhood made up of
      new housing units for low and moderate income
      families. The immediate neighborhood would
      be composed of families with roughly the same
      incomes, with the neighborhood residents
      having their own community facilities,
      including schools.
                                      _____
                                      3

11. If new housing were to be provided, which of the following two choices would you prefer?   __(47)

    a) Living together with members of all races   ____
                                                     1

                   or

    b) Living together with members of your own race   ____
                                                   2

PRESENT PICTURES OF MULTIPLE DWELLING UNITS

12. If you had a choice, which of the following housing units would you most like to live in? Second most? Least?

                    Picture #   Why

Most   ____   _____   __(48)

2nd most   ____   _____   __(49)

Least   ____   _____   __(50)

PRESENT PICTURES OF SINGLE DWELLING UNITS

13. If you had a choice, which of the following housing units would you most like to live in? Second most? Least?

                    Picture #   Why

Most   ____   _____   __(51)

2nd most   ____   _____   __(52)

Least   ____   _____   __(53)

JUST A FEW MORE QUESTIONS ABOUT YOUR HOUSEHOLD

14. Are you currently: __(54)

                              a) Single
                              b) Married   ____ 1
                              c) Divorced   ____ 2
                              d) Widowed   ____ 3
                                                   4

15. Head of household's age: (All female respondents without husbands are considered to be heads of their own households). __(55)

                              a) Under 30
                              b) 31-45   ____ 1
                              c) 46-60   ____ 2
                              d) 61 or older   ____ 3
                                                   4

16. What is the amount of money your household is currently living on, including wages of all members, welfare or aid to dependent children, social security, or unemployment payments:

```
Amount per week   $_____     Per week household income        __(56-
        or                   Under $50                            57)
Amount per month  $_____     $ 51-65              _____ 1
                               66-80              _____ 2
                               81-100             _____ 3
                              101-125             _____ 4
                              126-150             _____ 5
                              151-200             _____ 6
                             More than $200       _____ 7
                                                  _____ 8
```

17. Are you currently: __(58)

```
                    a) a non-registered voter      _____
                    b) a registered Independent    _____ 1
                    c) a registered Republican     _____ 2
                    d) a registered Democrat       _____ 3
                                                   _____ 4
```

INTERVIEWER PLEASE FILL IN RESPONDENT'S:

18. Sex: F___   M___   __(59)
              1   2

    Race: White___   Black___   Other___   __(60)
               1   2   3

Be sure to thank respondent very much and ask her/him if they would
like to make any generalized comments concerning the topics covered
by the questionnaire. Insert comments below:

Interviewer's Name:_____

Time of Day: Before 12:00noon___; 12:01-4:00p.m.___; 4:01-___   __(4)
                                 1   2   3

Day of Week: Mon__; Tue__; Wed__; Thu__; Fri__; Sat__; Sun__   __(5)
              1   2   3   4   5   6   7

Respondent's Neighborhood:_____   __(6)

Respondent Lives In: Multi-family____; Single-family____   __(7)
                             1   2

First call____; Call back_____

Hello! My name is _____ and I work for Gruen
Gruen + Associates, a research consulting firm. Lately there have
been many discussions concerning the impact of providing housing
for low and moderate income households in the suburbs. There are,
of course, numerous reactions to this issue. The purpose of this
survey is to get your honest reactions to a variety of alternatives
because we feel that it is important to take into consideration the
attitudes of people living in the community.

1. How long have you lived at your present address?_____   __(8-9)

1a. If single family, what type of mortgage do you have on your home.   __(10)
    Conventional__; V.A.__; FHA__; Cash__; Contract__; Land Bank__
              1   2   3   4   5   6

2. Please list all the factors which influenced your choice of a
    home in this location:

    _____   __(11)

    _____   __(12)

    _____   __(13)

    _____   __(14)

    _____   __(15)

    _____   __(16)

    _____   __(17)

3. Counting yourself, how many adults 18 years of age and older
    live in this household?_____   __(18)

4. How many children from 13-17 live in this household?_____   __(19)

5. How many children 7-12 live in this household?_____   __(20)

6. How many children 6 and under live in this household?_____   __(21)

7. Do you presently have any expectations of moving? Yes__ No__   __(22)
                                                         1   2

7a. Do you expect to move to: __(23)
    a) Another dwelling within this neighborhood?
                                                    _____
                                                       1

    b) Another neighborhood somewhere else in the
       community? Specify_____
                                                                2

    c) Another community somewhere else in this region?
       Specify_____
                                                               3

    d) Another region?_____
                                                               4

8. We are going to show you a series of pictures of different
    housing structures and would like to know how you feel they
    would 1) affect your neighborhood and 2) affect your community:

A Multi- family	Neighbor- hood Bene- fited Greatly	Neighbor- hood Some- what Bene- fited	Neighbor- hood Would Remain the Same	Neighbor- hood Would Be Somewhat Harmed	Neighbor- hood Would Be Greatly Harmed	
1	1	2	3	4	5	__(24)
2	1	2	3	4	5	__(25)
3	1	2	3	4	5	__(26)
4	1	2	3	4	5	__(27)
Single- family						
5	1	2	3	4	5	__(28)
6	1	2	3	4	5	__(29)
7	1	2	3	4	5	__(30)
8	1	2	3	4	5	__(31)

B. Multi- family	Community Benefited Greatly	Community Somewhat Benefited	Community Would Re- main Same	Community Would Be Somewhat Harmed	Community Would Be Greatly Harmed	
1	1	2	3	4	5	__(32)
2	1	2	3	4	5	__(33)
3	1	2	3	4	5	__(34)
4	1	2	3	4	5	__(35)
Single- family						
5	1	2	3	4	5	__(36)
6	1	2	3	4	5	__(37)
7	1	2	3	4	5	__(38)
8	1	2	3	4	5	__(39)

9. Which three structures would you least like to see locate
    in your neighborhood or community?

    __(40)
    __(41)
    __(42)

10. I am going to read you a list of statements and would like
    to know which are VERY IMPORTANT, IMPORTANT or UNIMPORTANT
    to your feeling these three structures would be harmful to
    your neighborhood or community:

	Very Im-portant	Im-portant	Unim-portant	
The structure is unattractive to me.	1	2	3	__(43)
The structure wouldn't fit in well with this area.	1	2	3	__(44)
Property values would decline if such structures were to be built here.	1	2	3	__(45)
Apartment units will lower the status of the neighborhood.	1	2	3	__(46)
Apartment buildings overtax such community services as water, sewage, police or fire.	1	2	3	__(47)
Apartment buildings overtax the community school system.	1	2	3	__(48)
Other (specify)_____ _____	1	2	3	__(49)

11. Although there is a tendency to lump all low and moderate
    housing assistance programs together, in actuality both the
    type of structures and type of households residing in that
    structure frequently differ. In addition to the above com-
    plexities, you may feel that a certain percent of each of
    these groups is a positive factor, while another percentage
    would exert either a neutral or negative influence on your
    neighborhood or community. We would like to have your re-
    actions to the provision of housing of the following percent
    levels and for the following household types, if this housing
    were to be constructed somewhere within your neighborhood. (See following page.)

179

01 Low Income White Elderly (Under $5,000)

	Greatly Improve Neighbor- hood	Improve Neighbor- hood Somewhat	Neighbor- hood Would Remain the Same	Harm Neighbor- hood Somewhat	Harm Neighbor- hood Greatly	
One family in 20	1	2	3	4	5	__(50)
One family in 10	1	2	3	4	5	__(51)
One family in 5	1	2	3	4	5	__(52)

02 Low Income Black Elderly (Under $5,000)

	Greatly Improve Neighbor- hood	Improve Neighbor- hood Somewhat	Neighbor- hood Would Remain the Same	Harm Neighbor- hood Somewhat	Harm Neighbor- hood Greatly	
One family in 20	1	2	3	4	5	__(53)
One family in 10	1	2	3	4	5	__(54)
One family in 5	1	2	3	4	5	__(55)

03 Low Income White Physically Handicapped (Under $5,000)

	Greatly Improve Neighbor- hood	Improve Neighbor- hood Somewhat	Neighbor- hood Would Remain the Same	Harm Neighbor- hood Somewhat	Harm Neighbor- hood Greatly	
One family in 20	1	2	3	4	5	__(56)
One family in 10	1	2	3	4	5	__(57)
One family in 5	1	2	3	4	5	__(58)

04 Low Income Black Physically Handicapped (Under $5,000)

	Greatly Improve Neighbor- hood	Improve Neighbor- hood Somewhat	Neighbor- hood Would Remain the Same	Harm Neighbor- hood Somewhat	Harm Neighbor- hood Greatly	
One family in 20	1	2	3	4	5	__(59)
One family in 10	1	2	3	4	5	__(60)
One family in 5	1	2	3	4	5	__(61)

05 Low Income White Family with Husband (Under $5,000)

	Greatly Improve Neighbor- hood	Improve Neighbor- hood Somewhat	Neighbor- hood Would Remain the Same	Harm Neighbor- hood Somewhat	Harm Neighbor- hood Greatly	
One family in 20	1	2	3	4	5	__(62)
One family in 10	1	2	3	4	5	__(63)
One family in 5	1	2	3	4	5	__(64)

06 Low Income White Family without Husband (Under $5,000)

	Greatly Improve Neighbor- hood	Improve Neighbor- hood Somewhat	Neighbor- hood Would Remain the Same	Harm Neighbor- hood Somewhat	Harm Neighbor- hood Greatly	
One family in 20	1	2	3	4	5	__(65)
One family in 10	1	2	3	4	5	__(66)
One family in 5	1	2	3	4	5	__(67)

07 Low Income Black Family with Husband (Under $5,000)

	Greatly Improve Neighbor- hood	Improve Neighbor- hood Somewhat	Neighbor- hood Would Remain the Same	Harm Neighbor- hood Somewhat	Harm Neighbor- hood Greatly	
One family in 20	1	2	3	4	5	__(68)
One family in 10	1	2	3	4	5	__(69)
One family in 5	1	2	3	4	5	__(70)

08 Low Income Black Family with Husband (Under $5,000)

	Greatly Improve Neighbor- hood	Improve Neighbor- hood Somewhat	Neighbor- hood Would Remain the Same	Harm Neighbor- hood Somewhat	Harm Neighbor- hood Greatly	
One family in 20	1	2	3	4	5	__(71)
One family in 10	1	2	3	4	5	__(72)
One family in 5	1	2	3	4	5	__(73)

09 Moderate Income White Family with Husband ($5,000-$10,000)

	Greatly Improve Neighbor- hood	Improve Neighbor- hood Somewhat	Neighbor- hood Would Remain the Same	Harm Neighbor- hood Somewhat	Harm Neighbor- hood Greatly	
One family in 20	1	2	3	4	5	__(74)
One family in 10	1	2	3	4	5	__(75)
One family in 5	1	2	3	4	5	__(76)

Card II   __(1)
           __(2)
           __(3)
           __(4)

181

10 Moderate Income White Family without Husband ($5,000-$10,000)

	Greatly Improve Neighbor-hood	Improve Neighbor-hood Somewhat	Neighbor-hood Would Remain the Same	Harm Neighbor-hood Somewhat	Harm Neighbor-hood Greatly	
One family in 20	1	2	3	4	5	__(5)
One family in 10	1	2	3	4	5	__(6)
One family in 5	1	2	3	4	5	__(7)

11 Moderate Income Black Family with Husband ($5,000-$10,000)

	Greatly Improve Neighbor-hood	Improve Neighbor-hood Somewhat	Neighbor-hood Would Remain the Same	Harm Neighbor-hood Somewhat	Harm Neighbor-hood Greatly	
One family in 20	1	2	3	4	5	__(8)
One family in 10	1	2	3	4	5	__(9)
One family in 5	1	2	3	4	5	__(10)

12 Moderate Income Black Family without Husband ($5,000-$10,000)

	Greatly Improve Neighbor-hood	Improve Neighbor-hood Somewhat	Neighbor-hood Would Remain the Same	Harm Neighbor-hood Somewhat	Harm Neighbor-hood Greatly	
One family in 20	1	2	3	4	5	__(11)
One family in 10	1	2	3	4	5	__(12)
One family in 5	1	2	3	4	5	__(13)

If respondent has given three or more negative responses (numbers 4 or 5) to alternates 01-12 ask questions 13 and 14 below:

13 Which four household types would you least like living in your neighborhood or community?

Insert Household
Type Numbers

_____   __(14-15)
_____   __(16-17)
_____   __(18-19)
_____   __(20-21)

14 I am going to read you a list of statements and would like to
    know which are VERY IMPORTANT, IMPORTANT or UNIMPORTANT to
    your feeling these household types would be harmful to your
    neighborhood:

	Very Important	Important	Unimportant	
Property values would drop.	1	2	3	__(22)
Property taxes would increase due to need for increased services.	1	2	3	__(23)
Neighborhood would face a drop in social status.	1	2	3	__(24)
Neighborhood would become less stable.	1	2	3	__(25)
These people would not fit in with rest of community.	1	2	3	__(26)
Housing maintenance and condition would decrease.	1	2	3	__(27)
Decrease in law and order.	1	2	3	__(28)
Change in character of neighborhood with shopping facilities catering to new group's needs.	1	2	3	__(29)
Drop in the quality of schools.	1	2	3	__(30)
These people would be a bad influence on my family because they don't believe in same things we do.	1	2	3	__(31)
Other (specify)_____	1	2	3	__(32)

15 Which of the following two alternatives do you most prefer, and
    do you prefer the chosen alternative a great deal more, somewhat
    more, or just slightly more than the other?

Alternative 1 - A small number of low and moderate income
housing units built in each neighborhood so that these households are scattered throughout the larger community.

Great Deal More	Somewhat More	Slightly More	
_____ 1	_____ 2	_____ 3	__(33)

Alternative 2 - The low and moderate income units to be built
in a separate neighborhood within your larger community. The
neighborhood, however, would share in the use of the community's
services, facilities and school system.

Great Deal More	Somewhat More	Slightly More	
_____ 1	_____ 2	_____ 3	__(34)

16 We would like to know your degree of acceptance of the provision
    of low and moderate income housing in your neighborhood, if the
    provision of such housing would result in:

    A. The government paying for an improved physical plant as
    well as increasing the quality level of the education given
    to the children in your community.

Housing Provided to:	Greatly Accepting	Moderately Accepting	Indifferent to	Moderately Unaccepting	Greatly Unaccepting	
Low income white families with husbands	1	2	3	4	5	__(35)
Low income white families without husbands	1	2	3	4	5	__(36)
Low income black families with husbands	1	2	3	4	5	__(37)
Low income black families without husbands	1	2	3	4	5	__(38)
Moderate income white families with husbands	1	2	3	4	5	__(39)
Moderate income white families without husbands	1	2	3	4	5	__(40)
Moderate income black families with husbands	1	2	3	4	5	__(41)
Moderate income black families without husbands	1	2	3	4	5	__(42)

B. An assurance that crime and delinquency would not show any increase.

Housing Provided to:	Greatly Accepting	Moderately Accepting	Indifferent to	Moderately Unaccepting	Greatly Unaccepting	
Low income white families with husbands	1	2	3	4	5	__(43)
Low income white families without husbands	1	2	3	4	5	__(44)

Housing Provided to:	Greatly Accepting	Moderately Accepting	Indiffer- ent to	Moderate- ly Unac- cepting	Greatly Unac- cepting	
Low income black families with husbands	1	2	3	4	5	__(45)
Low income black families without busbands	1	2	3	4	5	__(46)
Moderate income white families with husbands	1	2	3	4	5	__(47)
Moderate income white families without husbands	1	2	3	4	5	__(48)
Moderate income black families with husband	1	2	3	4	5	__(49)
Moderate income black families without husband	1	2	3	4	5	__(50)

C. An assurance that the households residing in these new housing units would share your values, beliefs and attitudes toward family, work, religion and education.

Housing Provided to:	Greatly Accepting	Moderately Accepting	Indiffer- ent to	Moderate- ly Unac- cepting	Greatly Unac- cepting	
Low income white families with husbands and children	1	2	3	4	5	__(51)
Low income black families with husbands and children	1	2	3	4	5	__(52)
Moderate income white families with husbands and children	1	2	3	4	5	__(53)
Moderate income black families with husbands and children	1	2	3	4	5	__(54)
Low income white elderly	1	2	3	4	5	__(55)
Low income black elderly	1	2	3	4	5	__(56)

Housing Provided to:	Greatly Accepting	Moderately Accepting	Indiffer-ent to	Moderate-ly Unac-cepting	Greatly Unac-cepting	
Low income white physically handicapped	1	2	3	4	5	__(57)
Low income black physically handicapped	1	2	3	4	5	__(58)

D. An assurance that property values will be maintained.

Housing Provided to:	Greatly Accepting	Moderately Accepting	Indiffer-ent to	Moderate-ly Unac-cepting	Greatly Unac-cepting	
Low income white families with husbands	1	2	3	4	5	__(59)
Low income white families without husbands	1	2	3	4	5	__(60)
Low income black families with husbands	1	2	3	4	5	__(61)
Low income black families without husbands	1	2	3	4	5	__(62)
Moderate income white families with husbands	1	2	3	4	5	__(63)
Moderate income white families without husbands	1	2	3	4	5	__(64)
Moderate income black families with husbands	1	2	3	4	5	__(65)
Moderate income black families without husbands	1	2	3	4	5	__(66)
Low income white elderly	1	2	3	4	5	__(67)
Low income black elderly	1	2	3	4	5	__(68)
Low income white physically handicapped	1	2	3	4	5	__(69)
Low income black physically handicapped	1	2	3	4	5	__(70

E. A guaranteed increase in level of services, such as more frequent garbage collection, improved sanitation, water, fire and police protection without any increase in your property tax.

Housing Provided to:	Greatly Accepting	Moderately Accepting	Indiffer- ent to	Moderate- ly Unac- cepting	Greatly Unac- cepting	
Low income white families with husbands	1	2	3	4	5	__(5)
Low income white families without husbands	1	2	3	4	5	__(6)
Low income black families with husbands	1	2	3	4	5	__(7)
Low income black families without husbands	1	2	3	4	5	__(8)
Moderate income white families with husbands	1	2	3	4	5	__(9)
Moderate income white families without husbands	1	2	3	4	5	__(10)
Moderate income black families with husbands	1	2	3	4	5	__(11)
Moderate income black families without husbands	1	2	3	4	5	__(12)
Low income white elderly	1	2	3	4	5	__(13)
Low income black elderly	1	2	3	4	5	__(14)
Low income white physically handicapped	1	2	3	4	5	__(15)
Low income black physically handicapped	1	2	3	4	5	__(16)

We would like to ask just a few additional questions about your household:

1. Is the head of household: __(17)

Under 30 _____
                    1
31 - 45   _____
                    2
46 - 60   _____
                    3

61 or older _____
                    4

                                                                                 (18-
2. What is the occupation of head of household: __ 19)

Blue collar   _____01
White collar   _____02
Sales   _____03
Managerial/Administrative   _____04
Professional/Technical   _____05
Military Officer   _____06
Military Enlisted or Non-
commissioned Officer   _____07
Retired   _____08
Unemployed   _____09
Student   _____10

                                                                                 (20-
3. What was the last grade head of household completed in school: __ 21)

Elementary 0 - 4th   _____01
            5 - 8th   _____02
High school 1 - 3 years   _____03
High school graduate   _____04
Technical/Vocational/
Business School   _____05
College 1 - 3 years   _____06
College graduate   _____07
Post college graduate work   _____08
Graduate degree   _____09

4. Does your household contain more than one wage earner?   __(22)
                              Yes   _____
                              No   _____1
                                         2
If yes, is additional wage earner employed: __(23)
                        Part time   _____
                        Full time   _____1
                                         2

188

5. Please tell me the letter that corresponds to the total income before taxes of your family during 1969. This includes wages and salaries, business projects, net family income, pension, rent and any other income received by members of this family: __(24)

A	0	-	$ 5,999	_____
B	$6	-	9,999	1
C	10	-	14,999	2
D	15	-	19,999	3
E	20	-	24,999	4
F	25	-	and over	5
				6

6. Are you currently: __(25)

1)	a non-registered voter	_____
2)	a registered Independent	1
3)	a registered Republican	2
4)	a registered Democrat	3
		4

Interviewer: Please fill in respondent's:

Sex:	Male	_____	__(26)
		1	
	Female	_____	
		2	
Race:	White	_____	__(27)
		1	
	Black	_____	
		2	
	Other	_____	
		3	

Be sure to thank respondent very much and ask him/her if they would like to make any generalized comments concerning the topics covered by the questionnaire. For example, is there something else that they believe the government should do if it is going to have programs that enable low and moderate income families to live in the community?

Present comments below and/or on reverse:

For Question 16A through 16E the interviewers were instructed to accept additional responses if the interviewee was unwilling to select one of the initially suggested alternatives. The additional accepted responses all fall into one of the following two categories:
    Not Possible - which means that the respondent did not find the
                   provision of such a facilitator credible
    Governmental - which is the rejection of governmental sponsorship
                   of such programs.
In addition to these two there was still a small percent of those who refused to answer the questions and this was recorded as a "don't know".

APPENDIX

C

SUMMARY OF
THE SAMPLING
METHODOLOGY

THE SUBURBANITE SAMPLE

Four geographic areas were defined for interview purposes, based on the percentage of households in three income categories and the attitudinal climate present in the area. The four suburban areas were selected by staff members of the MVRPC.

Having selected the areas, the next step was to differentiate the households by income. Because of the lack of current income data by small area, the judgment of income had to be made by another method. The Board of Realtors' Deed Record Manuals for the years 1968 and 1969 were used for this purpose. These manuals list street name, street numbers, and conveyance fee for houses sold in those two years. The conveyance fee is easily converted to house price ($1 fee per $1,000 selling price).

Income and house price were correlated through use of a standard ratio table:*

——————————

*Urban Housing Market Analysis, U.S. Department of Housing and Urban Development, Sales Price-to-Income and Rent-to-Income Ratios, modified for the Dayton Area, December, 1966.

191

Annual Income	House Price
$10,000 - 15,000	$21,000 - 29,000
15,000 - 25,000	29,000 - 44,500
25,000 +	44,500 +

An equivalent rental figure was also calculated by using a base of 18 percent of monthly income:*

Annual Income	Monthly Rent
$10,000 - 15,000	$149 - 225
15,000 - 25,000	225 - 374
25,000 +	374

Then began the process of locating the streets in the appropriate house price ranges and coding them on maps for all four areas. After this work was completed, the task of choosing specific households for interviewing was undertaken. For this, a directory of streets and their numbers was used. Streets were listed by price range, and all numbers on those streets that could be assumed from the Deed Record Manual to fall into the appropriate house price range were listed as well. All the street addresses were then numbered sequentially, and a table of random numbers used to pull the sample households from the comprehensive list.

Twice the number of required sample households was drawn in this manner to provide a duplicate sample pool, which would be equivalent in terms of location, structure type, and income category. This duplicate sample was then used to make substitutions for households who refused to answer or who were not at homes after one callback. After the two samples were drawn (approximately 100 households in each of the three income brackets and in both structure types),

---

*Urban Housing Market Analysis, U.S. Department of Housing and Urban Development, Sales Price-to-Income and Rent-to-Income Ratios, modified for the Dayton Area, December, 1966.

the streets were listed in a schedule that would
make the interviewing as efficient as possible in
regard to travel time.

Location of apartment complexes required a more
varied effort. Vacancy studies, Chamber of Commerce
material, the telephone directory, and newspaper
advertisements were carefully scanned to get as comprehensive a list as possible. Zoning and land use
maps were used, also, to pinpoint areas of multifamily
structures. In addition, a thorough search was made
through the Transportation Coordinating Committee
dwelling unit count data to areas not otherwise
indicated. Information on rents and number of units
was gathered for all of the apartments, and a random
numbers table used to draw the sample. These complexes were then fit into the interviewing schedule.

The interviewers had far greater difficulty in
obtaining cooperation from apartment dwellers than
single-family households. In the suburbanite sample,
44 percent of the apartment households and 40 percent
of the single-family households had to be replaced
with equivalent households due to "not at homes"
after one callback and refusals. We make no claims
that the replaced households were equivalent in their
attitudes but only in terms of their income category,
structure type, and geographic location within the
region. The single-family households were more
frequently not at home, while the apartment dwellers
maintained a higher refusal rate. Twenty-nine percent
of the original low-/moderate-income sample had to
be replaced with similar household types, because
22 percent were not at home after one callback and
7 percent refused to be interviewed. The percent
of completed interviews for the suburbanite and low-
and moderate-income household samples are presented
below.

	Completed Interviews	Not At Home	Refusal	Total
Suburbanite Sample: Apartment Households	56	13	31	100

Single-family Households	60	26	14	100

Low-/Moderate-
  Income
Household
  Sample
	71	22	4	100

THE LOW/MODERATE INCOME
HOUSEHOLD SAMPLE

Low income was defined as households earning under $5,000 a year. Moderate income included those households falling within the $5,000-$10,000 category. Since these definitions are not based on per capita estimates, there are, no doubt, some households improperly categorized, due to their size.

The sample for households making under $5,000 a year was drawn originally at random from the DMHA waiting list. The list was found to work well for locating poor families in the black neighborhoods. However, in the white neighborhoods, the list was not as valid, for many of the houses were vacant or no longer in existence. Thus, it was decided to use another method for determining where to best locate white families in this income category.

The method chosen was that of identifying geographic concentrations of poor white households in the city of Dayton. Minnie Johnson of the MVRPC staff was queried about this subject, and she suggested we use the Burns-Jackson area and the Parkside Homes and Cliburn Manor public housing projects. Subsequently, a random sample of white low-income households was selected for interviewing in these three areas.

The sample of households in the $5,000-$10,000 yearly income category was drawn by using the Deed Record Manuals, as in the suburbanite sample. Using the ratio table, it was defined that persons in this income range would most likely buy homes in the price range of $12,000-$20,000. Therefore, the

Manuals were carefully examined, and those streets
on which houses in the appropriate price range
predominated were extracted. All houses in the
appropriate street number range were then listed
from the city directory, and a random sample was
taken from that list. This method was used for both
black and white households in this income bracket.

This method was not faultless, however, and
especially in the white areas, several of the sample
households were found to be in a higher-income
bracket than was designated for this moderate-income
group. Randomly selected alternates, therefore,
were used in order to obtain the required number of
interviews.

The resultant coverage of the low- and moderate-
income interviews included West Dayton, lower Dayton
View, and scattered areas in Northwest, East, and
South Dayton. The interviewing was completed with
little difficulty.

A DESCRIPTION
OF THE TWELVE MUTUALLY EXCLUSIVE
SUBURBAN CATEGORIES

Suburban Groupings	Life Style*	Income**	Age***
1	1	2	1
2	1	2	0
3	1	1	1
4	1	1	0
5	1	0	1
6	1	0	0
7	0	2	1
8	0	2	0
9	0	1	1
10	0	1	0
11	0	0	1
12	0	0	0

*Ideally, the life-style variable would have separated multi-family structure, childless, more than one wage earner households from single-family structure, children, one wager earner households. But, because households do not fall so neatly into these two mutually exclusive categories, the life-style variable was calculated as follows:

0 {
1 Multifamily, no children, more than one wage earner
2 Multifamily, children, more than one wage earner
3 Multifamily, no children, one wage earner
4 Single-family, no children, more than one wage earner

1 {
5 Multifamily, children, more than one wage earner
6 Single-family, no children, one wage earner
7 Single-family, children, more than one wage earner
8 Single-family, children, one wage earner.

**Household income:

        0 = $14,999 and under
        1 = $15,000-$24,999
        2 = $25,000 and over.

***Age of head of household:

        0 = 45 and under
        1 = over 45.

197

SUBURBAN REACTIONS
TO LOW/MODERATE INCOME GROUPS
AND PROGRAM FACILITATORS

Suburban Prototypes, Sample Size, and Standard Error of the Mean

Suburban Prototype	Number of Respondent Households in Each of the Twelve Suburban Prototypes	Standard Error of the Mean*
1. Single-Family, 25+, Over 45	10	.62
2. Single-Family, 25+, Under 45	6	.80
3. Single-Family, 16-24, Over 45	12	.56
4. Single-Family, 16-24, Under 45	25	.40
5. Single-Family, 15 and Under, Over 45	13	.54
6. Single-Family, 15 and Under, Under 45	27	.38
7. Multifamily, 25+, Over 45	27	.38
8. Multifamily, 25+, Under 45	6	.80
9. Multifamily, 16-24, Over 45	12	.56
10. Multifamily, 16-24, Under 45	14	.52
11. Multifamily, 15 and Under, Over 45	9	.66
12. Multifamily, 15 and Under, Under 45	37	.32

*The standard error is primarily a measure of sample variability, that is, of the variations that occur by chance because a sample rather than the entire population is surveyed. As calculated for this study, the standard error also partially measures the effect of response and enumeration errors, but it does not measure, as such, any systematic biases in the data. The chances are about 68 out of 100 that an estimate from the sample would differ from a complete census figure by less than the standard error. The chances are about 95 out of 100 that the difference would be less than twice the standard error.

Suburban Reactions to Low-/Moderate-Income Groups and Program Facilitators

(a)

Low-Income White Families

Suburban Prototype	Low-Income White Family--Husband								Low-Income White Family--No Husband							
	No Facilitators (Population Level)			With Facilitators					No Facilitators (Population Level)			With Facilitators				
	5 Per-cent	10 Per-cent	20 Per-cent	A	B	C	D	E	5 Per-cent	10 Per-cent	20 Per-cent	A	B	C	D	E
Single-Family, 25+, Over 45	3.65 -	3.82 -	4.12 -	3.13 =	2.56 =	2.20 +	2.56 =	2.67 =	3.94 -	4.06 -	4.35 -	3.33 =	3.00 =	n.a.	2.78 =	2.89 =
Single-Family, 25+, Under 45	3.22 =	3.67 -	4.00 -	2.67 =	2.33 +	2.60 =	3.20 =	2.80 =	2.67 =	3.89 -	4.10 -	3.00 =	3.67 =	n.a.	3.20 =	2.80 =
Single-Family, 16-24, Over 45	3.20 =	3.90 =	4.20 -	2.50 =	2.60 =	2.40 =	2.18 +	2.33 =	3.40 =	4.10 -	4.60 -	2.75 =	3.00 =	n.a.	2.36 +	2.92 =
Single-Family, 16-24, Under 45	3.66 -	4.00 -	4.31 -	3.00 =	2.72 =	2.80 =	2.94 =	2.93 =	3.76 -	4.21 -	4.45 -	3.37 =	3.17 =	n.a.	2.89 =	3.07 =
Single-Family, 15 and Under, Over 45	3.55 -	3.68 -	3.91 -	2.44 +	2.56 =	2.80 =	1.78 +	2.60 =	3.42 =	3.86 -	4.10 -	2.93 =	3.25 =	n.a.	2.32 =	2.90 =
Single-Family, 15 and Under, Under 45	3.18 =	3.58 -	3.98 -	2.44 +	2.61 =	2.30 +	2.24 +	2.13 +	3.38 =	3.88 -	4.16 -	2.56 =	2.70 =	n.a.	2.33 +	2.25 +
Multifamily, 25+, Over 45	3.63 -	3.89 -	4.11 -	2.86 =	2.57 =	2.50 +	2.33 +	2.36 +	3.74 =	3.95 -	3.67 -	3.14 =	2.65 =	n.a.	2.43 +	2.41 +
Multifamily, 25+, Under 45	3.32 =	3.32 =	4.33 -	3.00 =	2.50 =	2.40 =	2.50 =	2.40 +	3.33 =	3.67 -	4.38 -	3.00 =	2.50 =	n.a.	2.50 =	2.40 +
Multifamily, 16-24, Over 45	3.57 -	3.86 -	4.07 -	2.67 =	3.11 =	2.60 =	2.67 =	2.78 =	3.85 =	4.15 -	4.89 -	3.00 =	3.33 =	n.a.	2.89 =	3.00 =
Multifamily, 16-24, Under 45	3.40 =	4.00 -	4.40 -	3.43 =	2.27 +	2.30 +	2.17 +	2.46 +	3.70 -	4.10 -	4.40 -	3.56 =	2.45 +	n.a.	2.64 =	.62 =
Multifamily, 15 and Under, Over 45	3.44 =	3.47 =	3.78 -	2.14 +	2.00 +	2.30 +	2.14 +	2.17 +	3.44 =	3.67 -	3.89 -	2.29 +	2.29 +	n.a.	2.14 +	2.17 =
Multifamily, 15 and Under, Under 45	3.36 =	3.64 -	4.12 -	2.33 +	2.28 +	2.30 +	2.08 +	2.03 +	3.60 =	3.92 -	4.40 -	2.54 +	2.42 +	n.a.	2.17 +	2.14 +

Note: Definition of the scores: + equals mean score is positive (1.00-2.49); = equals mean score is neutral (2.50-3.50); and - equals mean score is negative (3.51-5.00). N.a. reflects questions not asked because programs to allevi- ate fears were not relevant to these low- and moderate-income groups.

Suburban Reactions to Low-/Moderate-Income Groups and Program Facilitators

(b)

Low-Income Black Families

Suburban Prototype	Low-Income Black Family--Husband								Low-Income Black Family--No Husband							
	No Facilitators Population Level			With Facilitators					No Facilitators Population Level			With Facilitators				
	5 Per-cent	10 Per-cent	20 Per-cent	A	B	C	D	E	5 Per-cent	10 Per-cent	20 Per-cent	A	B	C	D	E
Single-Family, 25+, Over 45	4.07 (-)	4.13 (-)	4.20 (-)	3.33 (=)	2.56 (-)	2.00 (+)	2.56 (-)	2.67 (-)	4.27 (-)	4.27 (-)	4.40 (-)	3.67 (-)	3.56 (-)	n.a.	3.11 (-)	3.22 (=)
Single-Family, 25+, Under 45	3.56 (-)	3.89 (-)	4.22 (-)	2.67 (=)	3.33 (-)	2.60 (=)	3.60 (-)	3.40 (+)	3.67 (-)	3.44 (-)	4.11 (-)	3.00 (=)	3.67 (-)	n.a.	3.60 (-)	3.40 (=)
Single-Family, 16-24, Over 45	3.50 (=)	4.30 (-)	4.70 (-)	2.88 (-)	3.20 (-)	3.00 (=)	2.55 (+)	2.42 (+)	3.80 (-)	4.30 (-)	4.70 (-)	3.38 (-)	3.44 (-)	n.a.	2.82 (-)	2.92 (=)
Single-Family, 16-24, Under 45	3.69 (-)	4.14 (-)	4.41 (-)	2.17 (+)	2.94 (-)	2.90 (=)	2.44 (+)	2.93 (=)	3.97 (-)	4.34 (-)	4.55 (-)	3.68 (-)	3.17 (-)	n.a.	2.89 (-)	3.07 (=)
Single-Family, 15 and Under, Over 45	3.57 (-)	3.71 (-)	4.05 (-)	2.50 (-)	2.63 (-)	2.80 (=)	2.22 (+)	2.60 (=)	3.80 (-)	4.05 (-)	4.30 (-)	3.00 (-)	3.25 (-)	n.a.	2.44 (+)	2.90 (=)
Single-Family, 15 and Under, Under 45	3.48 (=)	3.85 (-)	4.23 (-)	2.72 (=)	2.74 (=)	2.60 (=)	2.38 (+)	2.25 (+)	3.60 (-)	4.10 (-)	4.38 (-)	3.08 (=)	2.96 (=)	n.a.	2.38 (+)	2.50 (=)
Multifamily, 25+, Over 45	3.74 (-)	3.89 (-)	3.95 (-)	3.21 (=)	2.78 (=)	2.60 (=)	2.52 (+)	2.45 (+)	4.00 (-)	4.16 (-)	4.42 (-)	3.43 (=)	2.96 (=)	n.a.	2.55 (=)	2.55 (=)
Multifamily, 25+, Under 45	3.33 (-)	3.67 (-)	4.43 (-)	3.00 (=)	2.50 (=)	3.10 (=)	2.50 (=)	2.40 (+)	3.33 (-)	3.67 (-)	4.43 (-)	3.00 (=)	2.50 (=)	n.a.	2.50 (=)	2.40 (+)
Multifamily, 16-24, Over 45	3.93 (-)	4.29 (-)	4.50 (-)	3.25 (-)	3.67 (-)	2.00 (+)	3.33 (=)	3.56 (=)	4.36 (-)	4.57 (-)	4.71 (-)	3.58 (-)	3.89 (-)	n.a.	3.67 (-)	3.89 (=)
Multifamily, 16-24, Under 45	3.90 (-)	4.20 (-)	4.50 (-)	4.00 (-)	2.73 (=)	2.80 (=)	2.75 (=)	2.92 (=)	4.10 (-)	4.50 (-)	4.60 (-)	4.22 (-)	3.09 (=)	n.a.	2.92 (=)	3.23 (=)
Multifamily, 15 and Under, Over 45	3.56 (-)	3.78 (-)	4.00 (-)	2.29 (+)	2.14 (+)	2.30 (+)	2.14 (+)	2.50 (=)	3.56 (-)	3.78 (-)	4.00 (-)	2.29 (+)	2.57 (=)	n.a.	2.14 (+)	2.50 (=)
Multifamily, 15 and Under, Under 45	3.60 (-)	4.00 (-)	4.40 (-)	2.54 (+)	2.39 (+)	2.50 (+)	2.28 (+)	2.22 (+)	3.88 (-)	4.12 (-)	4.56 (+)	2.71 (+)	3.69 (-)	n.a.	2.36 (+)	2.33 (+)

Note: Definition of the scores: + equals mean score is positive (1.00-2.49); = equals mean score is neutral (2.50-3.50); and - equals mean score is negative (3.51-5.00). N.a. reflects questions not asked because programs to alleviate fears were not relevant to these low- and moderate-income groups.

APPENDIX TABLE 1 (Continued)

Suburban Reactions to Low-/Moderate-Income Groups and Program Facilitators

(c)

Moderate-Income White Families

Suburban Prototype	Moderate-Income White Family--Husband								Moderate-Income White Family--No Husband							
	No Facilitators Population Level			With Facilitators					No Facilitators Population Level			With Facilitators				
	5 Per-cent	10 Per-cent	20 Per-cent	A	B	C	D	E	5 Per-cent	10 Per-cent	20 Per-cent	A	B	C	D	E
Single-Family, 25+, Over 45	3.18 =	3.41 =	3.47 =	2.93 =	2.22 +	1.80 +	2.22 +	2.44 =	3.47 =	3.65 =	3.71 -	3.13 =	2.67 =	n.a.	2.44 +	2.67 =
Single-Family, 25+, Under 45	3.11 =	3.22 =	3.56 -	2.50 =	3.33 +	2.60 +	3.80 -	2.60 =	3.11 =	3.22 =	3.67 -	2.67 =	3.67 -	n.a.	3.20 =	3.00 =
Single-Family, 16-24, Over 45	3.10 =	3.30 =	3.55 =	2.25 +	2.33 +	2.20 +	1.90 +	2.08 +	3.20 =	3.30 =	3.50 =	2.38 +	2.67 =	n.a.	2.18 +	2.25 +
Single-Family, 16-24, Under 45	3.07 =	3.31 =	3.62 -	3.00 =	2.72 +	2.80 +	2.33 +	2.79 =	3.28 =	3.59 =	3.92 -	3.32 =	3.11 =	n.a.	2.67 =	2.93 =
Single-Family, 15 and Under, Over 45	3.27 =	3.36 =	3.41 =	1.69 +	1.88 +	2.00 +	1.80 +	1.90 +	3.38 =	3.52 -	3.76 -	2.47 +	2.88 =	n.a.	2.00 +	2.20 +
Single-Family, 15 and Under, Under 45	2.95 =	2.95 =	3.18 =	2.44 +	2.43 +	2.40 +	2.24 +	2.21 +	2.88 =	3.18 =	3.50 -	2.53 =	2.57 =	n.a.	2.29 +	2.29 +
Multifamily, 25+, Over 45	3.16 =	3.21 =	3.42 =	2.64 =	2.43 +	2.40 +	2.14 +	2.18 +	3.32 =	3.42 =	3.53 -	2.86 =	2.57 =	n.a.	2.33 +	2.27 +
Multifamily, 25+, Under 45	3.00 =	3.00 =	3.00 =	3.00 =	2.50 +	2.00 +	2.50 +	2.40 +	3.00 =	3.00 =	3.00 =	3.00 =	2.50 =	n.a.	2.50 +	2.40 +
Multifamily, 16-24, Over 45	3.21 =	3.43 =	3.64 -	2.67 =	2.89 +	1.70 +	2.44 +	2.44 +	3.50 -	3.79 -	3.93 -	3.68 -	3.11 =	n.a.	2.78 =	2.78 =
Multifamily, 16-24, Under 45	2.80 =	3.00 =	3.20 =	2.56 +	1.91 +	1.80 +	2.17 +	2.15 +	3.20 =	3.50 -	4.00 -	2.78 =	2.18 +	n.a.	2.25 +	2.31 =
Multifamily, 15 and Under, Over 45	3.22 =	3.33 =	3.56 -	2.14 +	1.86 +	2.30 +	2.14 +	2.33 +	3.22 =	3.56 -	3.67 -	2.14 +	2.00 +	n.a.	2.14 +	2.33 +
Multifamily, 15 and Under, Under 45	3.00 =	3.12 =	3.16 =	2.38 +	2.14 +	2.10 +	1.89 +	1.94 +	3.04 =	3.16 =	3.32 =	2.42 +	2.20 +	n.a.	2.00 +	2.06 +

Note: Definition of the scores: + equals mean score is positive (1.00-2.49); = equals mean score is neutral (2.50-3.50); and - equals mean score is negative (3.51-5.00). N.a. reflects questions not asked because programs to alleviate fears were not relevant to these low- and moderate-income groups.

APPENDIX TABLE 1 (Continued)

Suburban Reactions to Low-/Moderate-Income Groups and Program Facilitators

(d)

Suburban Prototype	Moderate-Income Black Families								Moderate-Income Black Family--No Husband							
	No Facilitators, Population Level			With Facilitators					No Facilitators, Population Level			With Facilitators				
	5 Per-cent	10 Per-cent	20 Per-cent	A	B	C	D	E	5 Per-cent	10 Per-cent	20 Per-cent	A	B	C	D	E
Single-Family, 25+, Over 45	3.73 -	3.73 -	3.67 -	3.07 =	2.56 =	2.00 +	2.44 +	2.56 =	3.93 -	3.93 -	3.93	3.25 =	3.44	n.a.	3.00 =	3.00 =
Single-Family, 25+, Under 45	3.22 =	3.44 =	4.33 -	2.67 =	3.33 =	2.60 =	3.40 =	3.40 =	3.33 =	3.78 -	4.11 -	3.50 =	3.67 -	n.a.	3.40 =	3.40 =
Single-Family, 16-24, Over 45	3.50 =	3.60 =	3.90 -	2.63 =	4.00 =	2.60 =	2.36 +	2.25 +	3.50 =	3.80 -	4.00 -	2.89 =	3.10 -	n.a.	2.64 =	2.33 +
Single-Family, 16-24, Under 45	3.38 -	3.59 -	4.00 -	3.05 =	2.78 =	2.80 =	2.33 +	2.79 =	3.55 -	3.83 -	4.17 -	3.80 -	3.22 -	n.a.	2.78 =	2.93 =
Single-Family, 15 and Under, Over 45	3.38 =	3.43 =	3.57 -	2.19 +	2.75 =	2.40 +	2.10 +	2.20 +	3.65 -	3.80 -	3.90 -	2.60 =	3.00 =	n.a.	2.50 =	2.50 =
Single-Family, 15 and Under, Under 45	3.15 =	3.33 =	3.60 -	2.64 =	2.52 =	2.50 =	2.29 +	2.29 +	3.40 =	3.65 -	3.90 -	2.83 =	3.39 =	n.a.	2.33 +	2.38 +
Multifamily, 25+, Over 45	3.15 =	3.58 -	3.79 -	2.93 =	2.74 =	2.50 =	2.52 +	2.41 +	3.58 -	3.74 -	3.89 -	3.29 =	2.87 =	n.a.	2.57 +	2.45 +
Multifamily, 25+, Under 45	3.00 =	3.00 =	3.00 =	3.00 =	2.50 =	2.00 +	2.50 =	2.40 +	3.00 =	3.00 =	3.00 =	2.25 +	2.50 =	n.a.	2.50 =	2.40 +
Multifamily, 16-24, Over 45	3.43 -	3.86 -	4.14 -	3.17 =	3.44 =	2.80 =	3.22 =	3.33 =	3.79 -	4.21 -	4.36 -	2.50 =	3.89 -	n.a.	3.89 -	3.67 -
Multifamily, 16-24, Under 45	3.40 =	4.00 -	4.20 -	3.44 =	2.18 +	2.00 +	2.33 +	2.77 =	3.90 -	4.00 -	4.40 -	3.15 =	2.64 =	n.a.	2.58 =	2.85 =
Multifamily, 15 and Under, Over 45	3.44 =	3.67 -	3.78 -	2.14 +	2.29 =	2.30 =	2.14 +	2.33 +	3.44 =	3.78 -	4.00 -	2.17 +	2.29 =	n.a.	2.14 +	2.33 +
Multifamily, 15 and Under, Under 45	3.04 =	3.28 =	3.44 =	2.42 +	2.14 +	2.40 +	2.03 +	2.06 +	3.20 =	3.56 -	3.80 -	2.67 +	2.31 =	n.a.	2.17 +	2.22 +

Note: Definition of the scores: + equals mean score is positive (1.00-2.49); = equals mean score is neutral (2.50-3.50); and - equals mean score is negative (3.51-5.00). N.a. reflects questions not asked because programs to alleviate fears were not relevant to these low- and moderate-income groups.

SUBURBAN REACTIONS
TO LOW INCOME GROUPS
AND FACILITATING PROGRAMS

Suburban Reactions to Low-Income Groups and Facilitating Programs

Household Type	Facilitator A-- Education			Facilitator B-- Crime			Facilitator C-- Values			Facilitator D-- Property Values			Facilitator E-- Services		
	Income	Age	Struc-ture	Income	Age	Struc-ture	Income	Age	Struc-ture	Income	Age	Struc-ture	Income	Age	Struc-ture
Low-Income White Family--Husband	.16	.18	.16	.12	.11	.21	.10	.12	.21	.15	.14	.17	.13	.16	.18
Low-Income White Family--No Husband	.21	.21	.18	.09	.16	.25	n.a.	n.a.	n.a.	.16	.15	.18	.13	.16	.15
Low-Income Black Family--Husband	.18	.17	.13	.11	.15	.18	.11	.12	.18	.15	.13	.14	.12	.13	.15
Low-Income Black Family--No Husband	.21	.19	.17	.13	.19	.22	n.a.	n.a.	n.a.	.18	.16	.14	.14	.15	.14
Moderate-Income White Family--Husband	.17	.16	.12	.10	.13	.20	.15	.12	.19	.17	.13	.12	.13	.14	.15
Moderate-Income White Family--No Husband	.21	.17	.13	.11	.14	.22	n.a.	n.a.	n.a.	.18	.14	.16	.15	.16	.12
Moderate-Income Black Family--Husband	.17	.14	.08	.13	.18	.15	.16	.13	.15	.18	.15	.18	.15	.14	.12
Moderate-Income Black Family--No Husband	.23	.19	.13	.16	.20	.22	n.a.	n.a.	n.a.	.19	.17	.17	.15	.15	.17
Low-Income White--Elderly	n.a.	n.a.	n.a.	n.a.	n.a.	n.a.	.12	.13	.20	.16	.13	.15	.12	.13	.15
Low-Income Black--Elderly	n.a.	n.a.	n.a.	n.a.	n.a.	n.a.	.13	.13	.18	.15	.13	.18	.14	.12	.17
Low-Income White-- Physically Handicapped	n.a.	n.a.	n.a.	n.a.	n.a.	n.a.	.11	.12	.23	.15	.13	.15	.12	.14	.16
Low-Income Black-- Physically Handicapped	n.a.	n.a.	n.a.	n.a.	n.a.	n.a.	.14	.13	.21	.15	.13	.18	.12	.13	.15

Note: Correlations between .13 and .16 are significant at the > .05 level but < .01, while correlations of .17 and above are significant at or > .01 level. N.a. reflects questions not asked because programs to alleviate fears were not relevant to these low- and moderate-income groups.

G

PUBLIC

OFFICIAL

QUESTIONNAIRE

Person interviewed _____

Date _____

1. How do you feel your community would accept the following new housing structures?

Structure types	Greatly Accepting	Moderately Accepting	Indifferent to	Moderately Unaccepting	Greatly Unaccepting
Owner-occupied single family houses					
Renter-occupied single family houses					
Free-standing low rise apartments					
Free-standing high rise apartments					
High rise projects					
Low rise projects					
Garden type apartments					
Townhouse apartments					

For all negative responses ask "why".

2. How do you feel your community would accept the following new household types provided they make up less than 10 percent of your community's population:

Household type	Greatly Accepting	Moderately Accepting	Indifferent to	Moderately Unaccepting	Greatly Unaccepting
Low income (Under $5,000) White elderly					
Low income (Under $5,000) Black elderly					
Low income (Under $5,000) White Physically handi-capped					
Low income (Under $5,000) Black Physically handi-capped					
Low income (Under $5,000) White family with husband					
Low income (Under $5,000) Black family with husband					
Low income (Under $5,000) White family without husband					
Low income (Under $5,000) Black family without husband					
Moderate income ($5-10,000) White family with husband					
Moderate income ($5-10,000) Black family with husband					
Moderate income ($5-10,000) White family with-out husband					
Moderate income ($5-10,000) Black family without husband					

3. How do you feel your community would accept the following new household types provided they make up more than 20 percent of your community's population:

Household type	Greatly Accepting	Moderately Accepting	Indifferent to	Moderately Unaccepting	Greatly Unaccepting
Low income (Under $5,000) White elderly					
Low income (Under $5,000) Black elderly					
Low income (Under $5,000) White Physically handi-capped					
Low income (Under $5,000) Black Physically handi-capped					
Low income (Under $5,000) White family with husband					
Low income (Under $5,000) Black family with husband					
Low income (Under $5,000) White family without husband					
Low income (Under ($5,000) Black family without husband					
Moderate income ($5-10,000) White family with husband					
Moderate income ($5-10,000) Black family with hsuband					
Moderate income ($5-10,000) White family without husband					
Moderate Income ($5-10,000) Black family without husband					

4. If negative response to questions 2 or 3:

I am going to read you a list of statements and would like to know which are VERY IMPORTANT, IMPORTANT or UNIMPORTANT to your feeling that this household type would be harmful to your community.

Statement	Very Important	Important	Unimportant
Property values would drop			
Property taxes would increase due to need for increased services			
Community would face drop in social status			
Community would become less stable			
These people would not fit in with rest of community			
Housing maintenance and condition would decrease			
Decrease in law and order			
Change in character of community with shopping facilities catering to new groups' needs			
Drop in quality of the schools			

Other - (specify)

5. Would you ENCOURAGE, DISCOURAGE, or TAKE NO POSITION on issues such as zoning and planning guidelines within your jurisdiction that will tend to promote the development of new housing partially financed by the following programs:

	Encourage	Discourage	Take No Position
Standard public housing in projects			
Scattered public housing			
Turnkey public housing			
FHA housing			
V.A. housing			
Conventional			
235 (subsidies for moderate income single family residences)			
236 (subsidies for moderate income multi-family residences)			

6. Which groups most influence your thinking on providing low and moderate income housing in your community?

7. Are there any other comments you would like to make on this subject?

212

September 2, 1970

Dear _____ :

Our firm is currently working with the Miami Valley
Regional Planning Commission staff on a two-phase
study of programs to provide suburban housing opportunities for low and moderate income families. This
research effort follows a detailed analysis by the
planning staff that made specific allocations of the
housing needs of low and moderate income households
to the suburban sub-areas of this five-county Ohio
region. The first phase of the work we are doing
now is a survey research program investigating the
reactions of three groups to various programs and
approaches for providing the needed low and moderate
income housing in the suburbs. The three groups are:
(a) a sample of low and moderate income households of
the type that would be living in the units, (b) a
sample of the present residents of four suburban subareas and (c) a sample of the regions' public officials, builders, real estate operators and brokers.

Not surprisingly, both the positive and negative
reactions of all three groups stem from their attitudes toward and expectations concerning the impact
of the following kinds of integration or mixing:

1.   Economic   - Households with widely diverging
                        incomes living in the same block,
                        neighborhood or community.

2.   Socio-Cultural   - Households with greatly differing
                        values and life styles (i.e.,
                        differing household types) living
                        in the same block, neighborhood
                        or community.

3.   Racial

4.   Structural   - Single-family and multi-unit
                        dwellings being mixed on the
                        same block, neighborhood or
                        community.

The second phase of our research will be directed
toward forecasting the impact of various programs
and approaches on the factors of concern to both the
local low and moderate income residents that are pre-
sumed to benefit from the provision of new housing
in the suburbs, and on the factors that are of concern to the present residents of the Miami Valley
suburbs. A portion of the analysis required in phase
two will, of course, utilize the information on local
attitudes and priorities now being generated by the
phase one research. We will also draw on published
reports of the impacts that have resulted from housing integration or mixing of one or more of the four
types listed above. But we find few documented
analyses of such impacts except for areas in very
rapid transitions - this is particularly true of
economic and socio-cultural housing integration; and
that is why we are writing you.

We would like to draw upon your knowledge and experience to help us find areas where such mixings have
occurred. If you know of economically, socially,
racially or structurally mixed residental areas in
the United States please tell us about them.

We would appreciate your filling out the enclosed
questionnaire. Please feel free to call me collect

if you have questions or would rather make your comments verbally.

Sincerely,

Claude Gruen
Principal Economist

CG:ek

Enclosure

LOW/MODERATE INCOME HOUSING QUESTIONNAIRE

We are writing you because of your housing expertise. This questionnaire is not meant to be a constraint on your answers but a guideline. We welcome any comments or opinions you may wish to offer. Please call Dr. Claude Gruen collect at (415) 433-7598 if you have any questions or would prefer commenting over the phone.

I.   Do you know of any residential areas that provide housing for low and moderate income households that contain a wide range of economically, socially or racially divergent residents and/or contain a variety of structural types?

Yes ( ) If so, please continue with Question II.

No ( ) If not, please feel free to comment.

II. Which of these would you list as the best example of such housing environments?

Name   Location

a.   What size area is it?

b.   What kinds and what degree of mixing or integration is represented by the area? If it is possible, would you state the degree of mixing or integration in percentage terms.

1. Economic (i.e., range of income dispersion)

2. Racial

3. Socio-Cultural (i.e., household types, ethnic groups, occupations)

4. Structural (building types)

c. Approximately how many dwelling units are contained in the area?

d. Would you provide a short description of the area.

e. Would you describe the area or areas that surround it if housing is one of the adjacent uses; how does it compare on type, price and quality to the nominated area?

f. Please comment on or discuss the following:

How well do you think this area has succeeded in mixing groups and structural types? In what ways has it been successful? In what ways has it been a failure? How stable do you think the present mix is? What do you think the future make-up of the area will be? What impact has the general area had on the larger community?

g. If you have any other information about the area we would appreciate your mailing it to us. If not, where can we write or call to get more information about the area?

THANK YOU VERY MUCH FOR YOUR COOPERATION

Name of Area or Development: Lower East Side in vicinity of Chatham Square.

Location: New York.

Size of Area: No answer.

Type of Development: No answer.

Number of Total Units in Development: 2,000-3,000.

Economic Mix: Low to upper middle.

Sociocultural Mix: Chinese, Italian, Greek, Puerto Rican, black,
                                   Christian, Jew, Anglo-Saxon.

Racial Mix: White, black, Oriental.

Structural Mix: High-rise, 8 to 25 stories. Few 2 to 3-story
                                   brownstones.

Degree of Success in Mixing: No answer.

Name of Area or Development: Uniondale.

Location: Long Island, New York.

Size of Area: 4,298 acres.

Type of Development: Tract type, single-family housing.

Number of Total Units in Development: 11,000 dwelling units.

Economic Mix: $7,000-$12,000.

Sociocultural Mix: No answer.

Racial Mix: 11 percent black.

Structural Mix: Apartments to 7 stories and single-family
                                   houses.

Degree of Success in Mixing: No housing mix but racial mixture that
                                   appears to be stable.

Name of Area or Development: Hempstead.

Location: Long Island, New York.

Size of Area: 2,031 acres.

Type of Development: Single-family housing and apartments, some
                                   to 7 stories.

Number of Total Units in Development: 6,000 dwelling units.

Economic Mix: $7,000-$12,000.

Sociocultural Mix: No answer.

Racial Mix: 78 percent black.

Structural Mix: Single-family tract housing.

Degree of Success in Mixing: Structure types well mixed but area is
                                   turning black.

Name of Area or Development:	Mount Airy Neighborhood.
Location:	Philadelphia, Pennsylvania.
Size of Area:	37,619 population in 1966.
Type of Development:	No answer.
Number of Total Units in Development:	15,000.
Economic Mix:	1966: $3,000--27.5 percent; $3,000-$10,000-- 46.8 percent; over $10,000--25.6 percent.
Sociocultural Mix:	Extremely heterogeneous. Many middle-class blacks. Poor blacks, poor whites. Liberal white couples and white elderly.
Racial Mix:	60 percent black, 40 percent white.
Structural Mix:	Single-family before 1930. Philadelphia row houses. Mid- and high-rise apartments.
Degree of Success in Mixing:	Community associations active. Families moving into large homes send children to private schools.

Name of Area or Development:	Mount Airy Neighborhood.
Location:	Philadelphia, Pennsylvania.
Size of Area:	No answer.
Type of Development:	No answer.
Number of Total Units in Development:	$5,000-$10,000.
Economic Mix:	5 percent welfare, 40 percent over $20,000, rest in between.
Sociocultural Mix:	No answer.
Racial Mix:	30-40 percent black.
Structural Mix:	Apartments, row houses.
Degree of Success in Mixing:	States example of nationally known example of successful integration.

Name of Area or Development:	Germantown.
Location:	Philadelphia, Pennsylvania.
Size of Area:	56,877 population in 1966.
Type of Development:	No answer.
Number of Total Units in Development:	24,000.
Economic Mix:	No answer.
Sociocultural Mix:	No answer.
Racial Mix:	No answer.
Structural Mix:	No answer.
Degree of Success in Mixing:	No answer.

Name of Area or Development:	South End Neighborhood.
Location:	Boston, Massachusetts.
Size of Area:	600 acres +.
Type of Development:	Redevelopment area.
Number of Total Units in Development:	No answer.
Economic Mix:	0-$50,000+.
Sociocultural Mix:	Wide spectrum.
Racial Mix:	Black, white, Chinese, Puerto Rican.
Structural Mix:	Primarily low-rise houses.
Degree of Success in Mixing:	No answer.

Name of Area or Development:	Columbia.
Location:	Between Baltimore, Maryland, and Washington, D.C..
Size of Area:	7 villages. Each village contains 12,000 to 15,000.
Type of Development:	221D-3, 235 and 236 will eventually make up one-third of community.
Number of Total Units in Development:	Approximately 10 percent complete.
Economic Mix:	$6,000-$40,000. Most in $12,000-$16,000 range.
Sociocultural Mix:	No welfare or aid-to-dependent children families. Lower moderate-income households consist of younger households of similar class.
Racial Mix:	Approximately 15 percent black. Columbia deliberately does not keep records on racial mix so their salesmen will not be able to reveal this information when asked.
Structural Mix:	Townhouse garden apartments.
Degree of Success in Mixing:	There is very little class integration. The lower-income 235-256 households are either young couples, secretaries, or divorcees. Racial mix has been no problem.

Name of Area or Development:	Reston-Cedar Ridge.
Location:	Reston, Virginia.
Size of Area:	7,400 acres.
Type of Development:	198 units. 100 2-bedroom units, ranging from $120-$126 per month. 54 3-bedroom at $150 per month. 10 units set aside for public housing. A total of 440 moderate income units are in advanced planning stages. 240 under 236 program.
Number of Total Units in Development:	8,000.

Economic Mix: No low income. Moderate to upper middle.

Sociocultural Mix: Moderate-income housing has been primarily
                                                     attracting families.

Racial Mix: No answer.

Structural Mix: Houses, townhouses, apartments.

Degree of Success in Mixing: No answer.

Name of Area or Development: Lafayette-Elmwood Area.

Location: Downtown Detroit, Michigan.

Size of Area: Total area--692 acres. Lafayette Park, which
                                                     accounts for 2 out of 5 segments, is 193 acres.

Type of Development: Redevelopment area 221D-3, 235 and 236.

Number of Total Units in Development: 3,473 completed units for total area. 1,717
                                                     completed units in Lafayette Park.

Economic Mix: Rent levels: $70 to $100--senior citizens
                                                     apartments, $150--studio apartments, $300
                                                     townhouses.

Sociocultural Mix: Currently few low-income households. There
                                                     will be low-income households moving into
                                                     Elmwood II and III, which are currently
                                                     under construction.

Racial Mix: 19 percent black in low-rise apartments. 10
                                                     percent black in high-rise apartments.

Structural Mix: Townhouses, low- and high-rise apartments.

Degree of Success in Mixing: Lafayette is currently integrated by race but
                                                     not by class. Middle-class parents send
                                                     their children to all the public schools,
                                                     with one exception--an elementary school
                                                     serving a lower-income community.

Name of Area or Development: River Acres.

Location: Mt. Clemens, Michigan.

Size of Area: 160 acres.

Type of Development: Redevelopment-urban renewal area. (20) 235, (20)
                                                     scattered public housing.

Number of Total Units in Development: 450.

Economic Mix: No answer.

Sociocultural Mix: Mix of professionals, tradespeople in own businesses,
                                                     clerical, factory and welfare.

Racial Mix: 95 percent black.

Structural Mix: Most buildings less than 15 years old, older build-
                                                     ings rehabilitated. $40,000 ranch to moderate
                                                     priced colonials and trilevels.

Degree of Success in Mixing: Feels that black "showcase" community good. provides wide variety of housing for blacks and helps show others that black homeowners care about where they live. Little interaction with larger community.

Name of Area or Development:	Hyde Park-Kenwood.
Location:	Chicago, Illinois.
Size of Area:	55,000 population--2 square miles.
Type of Development:	Conventional.
Number of Total Units in Development:	No answer.
Economic Mix:	Moderate to high income. Few low income.
Sociocultural Mix:	Occupational diversity from blue collar to professional, university personnel, and retirees.
Racial Mix:	38 percent black--reduced from 49 percent in 1960.
Structural Mix:	Single-family houses, townhouses, low- rise apartments, 10 to 15-story apartment build
Degree of Success in Mixing:	Census tracts are biracial but vary from 99 percent white in one census tract to 96 percent black in another. Very little social interaction between racial groups. Joint participation of all households in community facilities. Local high school has gone from 60-40 black-white ratio to 75-25 percent in recent years. University of Chicago spends $300,000 annually to assure private police protection to protect Hyde Park. Crime rate in area has dropped 50 percent.

Name of Area or Development:	South Commons.
Location:	Chicago, Illinois.
Size of Area:	No answer.
Type of Development:	220, 221D-3.
Number of Total Units in Development:	3,000.
Economic Mix:	Diverse mix.
Sociocultural Mix:	No answer.
Racial Mix:	50 percent black.
Structural Mix:	Wide variety.
Degree of Success in Mixing:	No answer.

Name of Area or Development:	Lake Village.
Location:	Chicago, Illinois.

Size of Area: No answer.

Type of Development: 221D-3, 220, 236, conventional.

Number of Total Units in Project: 1,400.

Economic Mix: Project currently in process of being rented--
                                                 no figures.

Sociocultural Mix: No answer.

Racial Mix: No answer.

Structural Mix: Wide variety.

Degree of Success in Mixing: Not been in existence long enough to answer.

Name of Area or Development: Lincoln Park Community.

Location: Chicago, Illinois.

Size of Area: 1,000 acres--83,000 persons.

Type of Development: Urban renewal project.

Number of Total Units in Development: 27,000.

Economic Mix: Aid-to-dependent children family to millionaires.

Sociocultural Mix: Retirees to corporate giants.

Racial Mix: 3 percent Black, 5 percent Oriental, 84 percent
                                                 Caucasian, 10 percent Spanish-speaking.

Structural Mix: Single-family to high-rise.

Degree of Success in Mixing: Families with school age children moving out due to
                                                 increase in gang activity. Increase in childless
                                                 population and single adults.

Name of Area or Development: Stone Keygate.

Location: Indianapolis, Indiana.

Size of Area: No answer.

Type of Development: 221D-3 coop--334 units rent for $93.50 per month.
                                                 336 units rent for $72.50 per month. Recently
                                                 obtained permission to use 100 apartments for
                                                 rent supplement. Some apartments will rent for
                                                 $22.50 per month.

Number of Total Units in Development: 680 2-bedroom garden apartments.

Economic Mix: Income ceilings $5,722.50 for one person.
                                                 $9,397.50 for six persons. Surcharge for persons
                                                 over income limit. With rent supplement program
                                                 getting applications from aid-to-dependent
                                                 children welfare families.

Sociocultural Mix: Fairly young families with children. Semiskilled
                                                 through blue collar workers. A very few semi-
                                                 professionals.

Racial Mix: 100 percent black.

Structural Mix:	All apartments.
Degree of Success in Mixing:	No answer.

Name of Area or Development:	River House Apartments.
Location:	Indianapolis, Indiana.
Size of Area:	No answer.
Type of Development:	221D-3 BMIR project consisting of two 12-story high-rise apartment buildings. 294 units: 49 1-bedroom $108, 204 2-bedroom $126, 44 3-bedroom $145.
Number of Total Units in Development:	297
Economic Mix:	$6,143 maximum for single person. $10,080 for six. No low income.
Sociocultural Mix:	Young singles, couples and families with children. Some semiretired.
Racial Mix:	88 percent black, 15 percent white.
Structural Mix:	All apartments.
Degree of Success in Mixing:	No answer.

Name and Area or Development:	Lynn Corporation.
Location:	Indianapolis, Indiana.
Size of Area:	No answer.
Type of Development:	Numerous walk-up apartments. Older rehabilitated buildings. Majority 2 bedrooms followed by equal number of 1 and 3 bedrooms. A few efficiencies. Efficiencies $79, 1-bedroom $107, 2-bedroom $118 to $125, 3-bedroom $138.
Number of Total Units in Development:	No answer.
Economic Mix:	40 percent of units in each building allowed for rent supplement. Residents living in building at time of acquisition eligible for sliding market rent--25 percent of gross income for rent. Rent supplement and basic rent income from $3,250 to $9,394.
Sociocultural Mix:	Quite a few elderly. Some young families. Most basic rent occupants are young families, with semiskilled or blue collar head of household.
Racial Mix:	65 percent black, 35 percent white.
Structural Mix:	Old apartment buildings. Low-income duplexes. Single-family dwellings. Rehabilitated Lynn apartment buildings.
Degree of Success in Mixing:	No answer.

Name of Area or Development:	Park Hill.
Location:	Northeast Denver, Colorado.
Size of Area:	4 square miles covering 5 census tracts. 490 city blocks.
Type of Development:	No answer.
Number of Total Units in Development:	11,939.
Economic Mix:	Welfare recipients to high income. Welfare 7 percent of community. Median income in 1959-- $7,456-$9,397. 25 percent of family heads high-status occupations.
Sociocultural Mix:	Young families to retired couples. Semiskilled to professional.
Racial Mix:	Between 37 percent to 40 percent black. 60 percent white.
Structural Mix:	Majority of dwelling units are homes. Some duplexes and walk-up apartments.
Degree of Success in Mixing:	Community organizations have helped stabilize neighborhood. Have worked to maintain a single-family area and to maintain quality of education. Professional families have begun to move back in.

Name of Area or Development:	San Jose.
Location:	San Jose, California.
Size of Area:	1 million people.
Type of Development:	Public housing, FHA, 235. $21,000 mortgage limit to $60,000-$70,000 class.
Number of Total Units in Development:	No answer.
Economic Mix:	Wide range.
Sociocultural Mix:	Wide range.
Racial Mix:	Caucasian, Mexican-American, black.
Structural Mix:	Wide range.
Degree of Success in Mixing:	No answer.

Name of Area or Development:	Diamond Heights. Glenridge is moderate income.
Location:	San Francisco, California.
Size of Development:	125-175 acres.
Type of Development:	Redevelopment, 236, 221D-3.
Number of Total Units in Development:	1,500.
Economic Mix:	Currently moderate to high middle. 236 project underway. 221D-3.
Sociocultural Mix:	Mostly families. Occupations: post office, social workers, clerical to lawyers.
Racial Mix:	White, black, Oriental, Spanish surname.
Structural Mix:	Homes, townhouses, obvious apartments limited.
Degree of Success in Mixing:	No low-income present. Successful in mixing moderate income with middle income. Moderate have been carefully screened. Sales slightly slow directly across from moderate-income units. Fourplexes made to look like two individual townhouses.

BIBLIOGRAPHY

BOOKS AND PAMPHLETS

Abrams, Charles. Forbidden Neighbors. New York:
    Harper & Row, 1955.

Babcock, Richard F. The Zoning Game. Madison,
    Milwaukee, and London: University of Wisconsin
    Press, 1969.

Bailey, Stephen K. Disruption in Urban Public Secon-
    dary Schools. Washington, D.C.: National
    Association of Secondary School Principals,
    November, 1970.

Berger, Bennett M. Working-Class Suburb: A Study
    of Auto Workers in Suburbia. Berkeley and Los
    Angeles: University of California Press, 1960.

Coleman, Richard P., and Neugarten, Bernice L. Social
    Status in the City. San Francisco: Jossey-Bass,
    Inc., November, 1970.

Commission on Race and Housing. Where Shall We Live.
    Berkeley: University of California Press, 1958.

deLeeuw, Frank. Operating Costs in Public Housing:
    A Financial Crisis. Washington, D.C.: The
    Urban Institute, 1969.

Denton, John H., ed. Race and Property. Berkeley:
    Diablo Press, 1964.

Deutsch, Morton, and Collins, Mary Evans. Interracial
    Housing. New York: Russell & Russell, 1968.

Dobriner, William M. Class in Suburbia. Englewood
    Cliffs, N.J.: Prentice-Hall, Inc., 1963.

Donaldson, Scott. *The Suburban Myth: A Historical Perspective*. New York and London: Columbia University Press, 1969.

Eudey, Elizabeth. *A Move to Home Ownership*. San Francisco: San Francisco Development Fund, December, 1970.

Gans, Herbert J. *The Levittowners: Ways of Life and Politics in a New Suburban Community*. New York: Vintage Books, 1969.

Grier, Eunice, and Grier, George. *The Impact of Race on Neighborhoods in the Metropolitan Setting*. Washington, D.C.: Washington Center for Metropolitan Studies, 1961.

_____. Privately Developed *Interracial Housing*. Berkeley and Los Angeles: University of California Press, 1960.

Hoyt, Homer. *The Structure and Growth of Residential Neighborhoods in American Cities*. Washington, D.C.: Federal Housing Administration, 1939.

Kornhauser, Arthur, Mager, Albert J., and Harold L. Sheppard. *When Labor Votes*. New York: University Books, 1956.

Lansing, John B., Marans, Robert W., and Robert B. Zehner. *Planned Residential Environments*. Ann Arbor: Braun-Brumfield, Inc., 1970.

Laurenti, Luigi. *Property Values and Race: Studies in Seven Cities*. Berkeley: University of California Press, 1960.

Mahood, H. R., and Angus, E. L. *Urban Politics and Problems: A Reader*. New York: Charles Sonbrers Sons, 1969.

Mayor's Committee for Community Renewal. "Integrated Housing in the Lafayette-Elmwood Area." Detroit: 1970.

Miami Valley Regional Planning Commission. "Housing
    Needs in the Miami Valley Region 1970-1975.
    Dayton. Ohio: MVRPC, June, 1970

_____. "A Housing Plan for the Miami Valley Region.
    Dayton. Ohio: MVRPC, July 1970

Miller, Herman P. Rich Man, Poor Man. New York:
    Thomas Y. Crowell Company, 1971.

National Committee Against Discrimination in Housing.
    How the Federal Government Builds Ghettoes. New
    York: October, 1968.

Pascal, A. H. The Economics of Housing Segregation.
    Memorandum RM-5510-RC. Santa Monica: The Rand
    Corporation, 1967.

Rapkin, Chester. Market Experience and Occupancy
    Patterns in Interracial Housing Developments.
    Philadelphia: University of Pennsylvania,
    Institute of Urban Studies, July, 1957.

Rapkin, Chester, and Grigsby, William G. The Demand
    for Housing in Racially Mixed Areas. Berkeley
    and Los Angeles: University of California Press,
    1960.

Rex, John, and Moore, Robert. Race, Community and
    Conflict. London and New York: Oxford Univer-
    sity Press, 1967.

Royer, Donald M. Attitudes of White and Negro Resi-
    dents Towards Living in Integrated Neighborhoods
    in Thirteen Indiana Communities. Indianapolis,
    Ind.: Civil Rights Commission, 1964.

San Francisco Planning and Urban Renewal Association.
    Report No. 49. San Francisco: August, 1970.

Seeley, John R., Sim, R. Alexander, and Elizabeth
    W. Loosley. Crestwood Heights: A Study of the
    Culture of Suburban Life. New York: John Wiley
    & Sons, Inc., 1963.

229

Smith, Wallace F. <u>Housing: The Social and Economic
     Elements</u>. Berkeley and Los Angeles: University
     of California Press, 1970.

U.S. Department of Commerce, Bureau of the Census.
     <u>Current Population Reports: Income in 1969 of
     Families and Persons in the U.S.</u> Series P-60,
     No. 75. Washington, D.C.: U.S. Government
     Printing Office, 1970.

_____. <u>Statistical Abstract of the United States</u>.
     91st ed.; Washington, D.C.: U.S. Government
     Printing Office, 1970.

Wilners, Daniel M. <u>The Housing Environment and
     Family Life</u>. Baltimore: Johns Hopkins Press,
     1962.

                    ARTICLES AND PAPERS

Aaron, Henry. "Income Taxes and Housing," <u>The Ameri-
     can Economic Review</u> (December, 1970).

Aronov, Edward. Member of the Executive Committee,
     The Potomac Chapter and the Workshop Committee,
     Potomac Chapter of NAHRO. Washington, D.C., March,
     1965.

Bailey, Martin V. "Effects of Race and Other Demo-
     graphic Factors of the Values of Single Family
     Homes," <u>Land Economics</u>, XLII, No. 2 (May, 1966),
     215-20.

Bauer, Catherine. "The Dreary Deadlock of Public
     Housing," <u>Architectural Forum</u> (May, 1957).

Blumberg, L., and Lalli, M. "Little Ghettoes: A
     Study of Negroes in the Suburbs," <u>Phylon</u> (Summer,
     1966), 117-31.

Brooks, Mary. "Exclusionary Zoning." American
     Society of Planning Officials Service Report
     No. 254 (1970).

Cass, James. "Education in America, The Crisis of
    Confidence--and Beyond," Saturday Review (Sep-
    tember 19, 1970), pp. 61-62.

Clark, E. E., and Jones, R. L. "Changes in Attitudes
    Toward a Low Rent (8) Housing Project, Journal
    of Applied Psychology, Vol. XL, 201-12.

Committee on Banking and Currency, Subcomittee on
    Housing and Urban Affairs. "Progress Report on
    Federal Housing and Urban Development Programs."
    Washington, D.C.: U.S. Government Printing Office,
    March, 1970.

Department of Housing and Urban Development. "Clip
    Sheet." July 27, 1970.

_____. Newsletter, I, No. 16 (September 15, 1970).

Downs, Anthony. "Alternative Forms of Future Urban
    Growth in the United States," Journal of the
    American Institute of Planners, XXXVI, No. 1
    (January, 1970), 3-11.

_____. "An Economic Analysis of Property Value
    and Race," Land Economics (May, 1960).

_____. "Housing the Urban Poor: The Economics
    of Various Strategies," The American Economic
    Review (September, 1969),646-51.

Economic Development Committee of Prince George's
    County, Maryland. "A Study of Income and
    Expenditures by Family Dwelling, Apartment and
    Business Units and Individual School Children
    for the Fiscal Year 1963-1964." Prince George's
    County Economic Development Committee:
    Hyattsville, Maryland, October, 1963.

Fielding, Byron. "Home Ownership for Low-Income
    Families," Journal of Housing, XXVI, No. 6
    (June, 1969) and No. 8 (August-September, 1969).

Fishman, Joshua A. "Some Social and Psychological
    Determinants of Intergroup Relations in Changing

231

Neighborhoods: An Introduction to the Bridgeview study," <u>Social Forces</u> (October, 1961),
42-51.

Gruen, Claude. "Urban Renewal's Role in the Genesis
of Tomorrow's Slums," <u>Land Economics</u>, XXXIX,
No. 3 (August 6, 1963).

Human Research Association. "Housing Needs and
Attitudes of a Selected Sample of Santa Clara
County Residents." Preliminary Draft. July
23, 1970.

Kristoff, Frank S. "Urban Housing Needs Through the
1980s, An Analysis and Projection." Research
Report No. 10. Washington, D.C.: The National
Commission on Urban Problems, 1968.

Ladd, W. M. "The Effect of Integration on Property
Values." <u>The American Economic Review</u> (September,
1962), 801-8.

Lane, Sylvia. "Housing the Underhoused," <u>The Annals
of Regional Science</u> (December, 1970), 68-79.

Lebergott, Stanley. "Slum Housing: A Proposal," <u>The
Journal of Political Economy</u>, LXXVIII, NO. 6
(November-December 1970), 1362-66.

Lieberson, Stanley. "The Impact of Residential
Segregation on Ethnic Assimilation," <u>Social
Forces</u> (October, 1961), 52-57.

Marcus, Matitzahu. "Racial Composition and Home
Price Changes: A Case Study," <u>American Institute
of Planners Journal</u> (September, 1968), 334-38.

McGuire, Marie. "New Patterns of Partnership Between
Public Housing Authorities and Non-Profit Sponsors." Presented at the Fourteenth Annual Meeting
of National Council on the Aging, Washington,
D.C., March 3, 1965.

Meer, Bernard and Freedman, Edward. "The Impact of Negro Neighbors on White Home Owners, Social Forces, XLV, No. 1 (September, 1966), 11-19.

Monroe, Allen L. "Xenia City School District Survey Report." Unpublished.

Muth, Richard. "The Urban Economy and Public Problems," Financing the Metropolis, Urban Affairs Annual Reviews IV (1970), 435-56.

Netzer, Dick. "Tax Structures and Their Impact on the Poor," Financing the Metropolis, Urban Affairs Annual Reviews, IV (1970), 459-79.

Nixon, Richard M. "Second Annual Report on National Housing Goals." House Document No. 91-292. Washington, D.C: U.S. Government Printing Office, 1970.

O'Bannon, Joan E. "Payments from Tax-Exempt Property," Property Taxation-USA. Madison, Milwaukee, and London: The University of Wisconsin Press, (1969), 187-212.

Osenbaugh, Charles L. "Integrated Housing and Value," Appraisal Journal (January, 1967), 17-21.

Palmore, Erdman. "Integration and Property Values in Washington, D.C," Phylon (Spring, 1966), 15-19.

Pascal, Anthony H. "The Analysis of Residential Segregation," Financing the Metropolis, Urban Affairs Annual Reviews, IV (1970), 401-34.

Rose, Arnold, and Warshay, Leon. "Inconsistencies in Attitudes Toward Negro Housing," Social Problems (Spring, 1961), 286-92.

Santa Clara Planning Department. "Tenant-Landlord Problems/Recommendations." Unpublished.

Schrag, Peter. "End of the Impossible Dream,"
    Saturday Review (September 19, 1970), 68-96.

Slitor, Richard E. "The Federal Income Tax in Relation
    to Housing." Research Report No. 5. Washington,
    D.C.: The National Commission on Urban Problems,
    1968.

_____. "The Tipping-Point in Racially Changing
    Neighborhoods," American Institute of Planners
    Journal (August, 1963), 217-22.

Tipps, Paul. "Probable Effect of Public Housing on
    Selected School Districts." June, 1969. Un-
    published.

Wheaton, William L. C. Architectural Forum (June, 1967),
    141.

NINA JAFFE GRUEN is the principal sociologist
for Gruen Gruen + Associates. Prior to forming the
company, Mrs. Gruen was an independent consultant
specializing in urban sociology, marketing, and survey
research. She has designed and directed a broad
variety of studies that have required the utilization
of survey research and sociological techniques to
probe into the attitudes, motivations, preferences,
and behavior of important groups. She is a pioneer
in the synthesizing of behavioral research information
with time-series data in order to forecast market
and social reactions to presently unavailable service
and product options.

Mrs. Gruen has been, formerly, on the faculties
of the University of Cincinnati and the University
of Kentucky in Covington. She has also been a guest
lecturer at the University of California at Berkeley.

Mrs. Gruen received her B.A. with high honors
and her M.A. in Psychology from the University of
Cincinnati, where she was elected to membership in
Phi Beta Kappa.

CLAUDE GRUEN is the principal economist of
Gruen Gruen + Associates. For six years prior to
forming his own company, Dr. Gruen directed research
assignments as a senior economist working for an
international research and consulting firm. Dr. Gruen
is an urban economist with extensive experience in the
fields of housing, land use, prearchitectural pro-
graming, transportation analysis, forecasting, and
economic modeling.

Since 1964, Dr. Gruen has served part-time on
the faculty of the University of California at Berkeley, teaching in the College of Environmental

Designs' Departments of Architecture and City and
Regional Planning and in the School of Business
Administration. In addition, he has worked as a
research economist at the University's Center for
Real Estate and Urban Economics.

    Dr. Gruen received both his M.A. and his Ph.D.
degrees in Economics from the University of Cincinnati,
where he also did work in urban planning.